Too many books about personal/emotional problems lead us
toward *shallow solutions* dressed in biblical
language or *secular solutions* that disregard biblical truth.
Dr. Carlson writes with a passion
for God and people that strikes the needed balance;
he points us toward a perspective that respects scientific data,
feels compassion for hurting people and
honors, above all else, God's Word.

LARRY CRABB,
author of Finding God *and*
director of the Institute of Biblical Counseling

Why Do Christians Shoot Their Wounded? is going
to help a lot of people who have been rejected and hopefully
prevent others from being victimized.

STEPHEN ARTERBURN,
founder, New Life Treatment Centers

Dr. Carlson's book will be a positive
contribution to a better understanding of the
relationship of mental health to our lives.

HAROLD J. SALA,
president, Guidelines International Ministries

Why Do Christians Shoot Their Wounded?

Helping (Not Hurting) Those with Emotional Difficulties

DWIGHT L. CARLSON, M.D.

INTERVARSITY PRESS
DOWNERS GROVE, ILLINOIS 60515

InterVarsity Press® is the book-publishing division of InterVarsity Christian Fellowship®, a student movement active on campus at hundreds of universities, colleges and schools of nursing in the United States of America, and a member movement of the International Fellowship of Evangelical Students. For information about local and regional activities, write Public Relations Dept., InterVarsity Christian Fellowship, 6400 Schroeder Rd., P.O. Box 7895, Madison, WI 53707-7895.

Unless otherwise indicated, Scripture taken from the New American Standard Bible, ©1960, 1962, 1963, 1971, 1972, 1973, 1975, 1977 by the Lockman Foundation. Used by permission.

Cover illustration: Robert Linkiewicz
Cover photograph: Michael Goss

ISBN 0-8308-1666-6

Printed in the United States of America

Library of Congress Cataloging-in-Publication Data

Carlson, Dwight L.

    Why do Christians shoot their wounded?: helping (not hurting)
those with emotional difficulties/Dwight L. Carlson.
      p.   cm.
    Includes bibliographical references.
    ISBN 0-8308-1666-6
    1. Church work with the mentally ill. 2. Psychiatry and religion.
3. Mental health—Religious aspects—Christianity. I. Title.
BV4461.C37   1993
259'.4—dc20   93-43019
                                                  CIP

15   14   13   12   11   10 9 8 7 6 5 4 3 2

05   04   03   02   01   00 99 98 97 96 95

There are legions of God-fearing Christians who—
to the best of their ability—
are walking according to the Scriptures
and yet are suffering from emotional symptoms.
Many of them have been judged for their condition
and given half-truths and clichés
by well-meaning but ill-informed fellow believers.
To these wounded
saints I dedicate this book.

Preface

I have been a Christian for fifty years, a physician for twenty-nine and a psychiatrist for fifteen. In my experience Christians are intolerant, if not prejudiced, against individuals with emotional difficulties. Most view all such problems as due to personal sin. Some well-known Christian authors have further fueled the fires of stigma and judgment toward those suffering with emotional illness.[1]

Upon returning from an overseas ministry serving missionaries, a dedicated Christian friend and psychologist said to me, "The only army that shoots its wounded is the Christian army." He found that the philosophy of one group of missionaries could be summed up in three steps:

1. We don't have emotional problems. If any emotional difficulties *appear* to arise, we simply deny (even to ourselves) having them.

2. If we fail to achieve the ideal of step one and become aware of a problem, then we won't *admit* to it. We strive to keep it from family members and *never* breathe a word of it outside the family.

3. If steps one and two both fail, then we still won't seek professional help.

This philosophy is not limited to one group of missionaries; it illustrates an attitude I have seen throughout Christendom. It occurs among lay leaders, pastors, priests, charismatics, fundamentalists and evangeli-

---

[1]Throughout this book I use "emotional symptoms," "difficulties" and "problems" interchangeably. Sometimes I use these instead of "emotional illness," "mental illness" or "disease."

cals alike. Furthermore, the toll taken by emotional illness seems to permeate the ranks of all these groups equally.

This book examines the problem of emotional illness and, in particular, why many Christians treat the emotionally ill as sinners instead of wounded saints who need a helping hand. It looks, in the light of the Scriptures, at the vast number of recent scientific studies on the causes of emotional difficulties. It concludes with practical suggestions for the church, its leaders, the emotionally healthy people and those suffering with emotional symptoms.

All the incidents portrayed throughout the book are real; however, names and minor details have been changed to protect the individuals. In some instances the person I describe is a composite of several people.

I want to thank a number of patients, friends and colleagues who critiqued this manuscript for me. In addition, Fritz Ridenour gave some very helpful suggestions and Dr. Jambur Ananth, professor of psychiatry at UCLA, double-checked the medical accuracy of the material. Don and Shirley Durran graciously allowed us to use their cabin and Mike and Roz Halikis their condo as hideaways to write. I am deeply indebted to my daughter, Susan Carlson Wood, and my wife, Betty, for their tireless help in editing and typing this book.

PART I

How and Why
We Shoot
the Wounded

P ERHAPS YOU'VE HEARD SOMEONE JOKINGLY REMARK, "ONLY CHRISTIANS shoot their wounded!"

But it's no joke; it's true—particularly when emotional illness is involved. An attitude permeating much of Christianity assumes that emotional problems are almost always due to deliberate sin or bad choices (often considered sinful as well). In chapter one I introduce you to some of the wounded. In chapters two and three I explain why many Christians, including prominent leaders and authors, keep shooting them.

— 1 —

Don't Shoot! I'm Already Wounded!

A THIRTY-EIGHT-YEAR-OLD DEDICATED CHRISTIAN, WHOM I'LL CALL MARY, sat in my office crying. "Down" days had plagued her for years, but in the last six months she had become increasingly depressed; a persistent cloud of doom hung over her head. She felt as if she was "in hell"—as if God was punishing her. She felt guilty, and the long sleepless nights left her exhausted all day. To eat was a chore; to concentrate was next to impossible. She spent more and more time in Bible study and prayer, hoping that would help, but it didn't. The Scriptures seemed to condemn her, and her prayers bounced off the ceiling. She couldn't get away from the agonizing pain of depression.

Mary's husband, a deacon in the church, didn't understand why she couldn't just "snap out of it." Her Bible study leader simply asked, "Have you confessed your sin of depression yet?" Mary felt too wounded to explain her situation. She had cried to God repeatedly to forgive her of all sin, even though she wasn't able to pinpoint any—but a vague feeling persisted: *you must be sinning or you wouldn't feel this way.* She wondered if this attitude toward her illness might have come from a Christian book about depression. It said, "If a person has 'the peace of God which passeth all understanding' (Philippians 4:7) in his life he cannot have emotional conflict. Ultimately . . . symptoms are spiritual problems."[1]

She visited the church of a popular TV pastor and went forward for healing. While waiting in line, someone in front of her asked the well-known minister for help with her depression. The minister told the lady, "I won't pray for you, because depressed people feel sorry for themselves and God doesn't condone that." This shocked Mary so that she left immediately, feeling much worse and very confused. Her own pastor also failed to understand the depth of her problem.

For months she struggled with the pros and cons of seeking professional help. Her husband opposed such treatment because the main speaker at a Christian conference center had said, "If you are a committed Christian you shouldn't need a psychiatrist." Five times she started to dial my number before she had the courage to complete the call. As she sat in my office, tears streamed down her face; the underlying depression had grown to suicidal proportions. On top of this, she felt guilty for not being able to solve the problem on her own. Convinced that sitting in my office made her a failure, she concluded, "I *shouldn't* feel this way."

*   *   *

Charles is a conscientious attorney who, after losing an important case, began to have severe panic attacks. His heart pounded so hard that he was convinced he would soon die of a heart attack, have a severe stroke or go crazy. He broke out in a cold sweat, felt a prickly-tingling sensation throughout his body, became light-headed and believed everyone could see how frightened he was. At first this terror hit him when he tried to go back to court; then it started when he went to the office. His wife responded angrily: "It's all emotional—just get ahold of yourself."

*   *   *

Skip, a twenty-year-old minister's son, was president of his high-school class and, until last year, active in his church youth group. Then his college grades began to drop, and he found it nearly impossible to concentrate on his studies. He began hearing voices and became terrified that people were out to hurt him. He became overwhelmed with what was happening to him and the world around him. He was diagnosed as having schizophrenia, and medications brought him much relief. His hallucinations and suspicion of others stopped, but he was not able to resume his classes.

His father had just finished reading a book on spiritual warfare. It said, "The obvious psychological illness to relate to demonic activity is schizophrenia."[2] So the elders prayed for Skip, and his dad insisted that he not take the "drugs." But the result confused Skip: when he didn't take the medication, the horrifying voices returned, telling him to protect himself before someone killed him. Now he is so fearful that he carries a knife for protection.

"It's Just a Sin Problem"

With their inability to find relief, is it any wonder that the advice received by Mary, Charles and Skip only confused them?

Many Christians, including prominent leaders, view most if not all emotional problems as the direct result of personal sin or bad choices. I have been told that such individuals "just have a sin problem." Dwight Pentecost, in his book *Man's Problems—God's Answers,* says, "Thus we must first of all honestly face this fact that when we give way to worry, anxious care, and concern, we are disobeying a specific command of Scripture given by God to His children, and we are displeasing Him because of our sin."[3] Statements such as this are not uncommon. Turn on the radio or TV, or pick up one of many current Christian books and you will find any negative emotion pronounced a sin, whether it is anger, doubt, depression or anxiety.

Beyond Seduction by Dave Hunt is an example of such a book. He says, "There is no such thing as a *mental* illness; it is either a physical problem in the brain (such as a chemical imbalance or nutritional deficiency) or it is a moral or *spiritual* problem."[4] John MacArthur, in *Our Sufficiency in Christ: Three Deadly Influences That Undermine*

Your Spiritual Life, takes a similar position, saying that "there may also be certain types of emotional illnesses where root causes are organic," but adding that "these are relatively rare problems. . . . Every need of the human soul is ultimately spiritual. There is no such thing as a 'psychological problem' unrelated to spiritual or physical causes. God supplies divine resources sufficient to meet all those needs completely." Referring to those who seek psychological help he concludes: "Scripture hasn't failed them—they've failed Scripture."[5]

These spokesmen represent a large segment of Christianity that judges virtually all mental and emotional problems as due to deliberate sin of the individual. With such a conclusion it is understandable how they would deeply wound those suffering with emotional symptoms.

"No One Who Is Right with the Lord Has a Nervous Breakdown"

People who believe that emotional problems are caused by one's sin will inevitably communicate to others that it's *not* O.K. to have emotional problems. Sometimes we are as judgmental as Job's "friends" or the Pharisees in conveying that the person going through a difficult time is sinning. For example, Eliphaz told Job, "Stop and think! Have you ever known a truly good and innocent person who was punished? . . . My advice to you is this: Go to God and confess your sins" (Job 4:7, 5:8 LB). This judgment adds a giant burden to the person who is already struggling with a heavy load.

Harold Sala of Guidelines International Ministries recently wrote to me about a colleague of his, whom I'll call Sam. While teaching and working on his doctorate, Sam had some major concerns about how a specific Christian university was spending significant amounts of its money. After looking into the matter, he became convinced that unethical practices were being employed which he couldn't condone. He felt he needed to resign his teaching position, even though he knew the university would probably blackball him so that he wouldn't be able to get a teaching position elsewhere. The tension began to eat away at him, pushing him to the brink of a nervous breakdown.

When he checked into the university hospital for a few days of rest with medication, the university president told the student body, "Nobody who is right with the Lord has a nervous breakdown and needs medication." This statement, of course, got back to the individual who had served the university with distinction for many years.

Feeling completely trapped and that his life had become unbearable, Sam took a .22 pistol, shot himself in the stomach, and bled to death over a period of hours. The response of the university? It refused to let either the students or his fellow professors attend the funeral! This event took place in the 1960s, but the position regarding mental illness held by that fundamentalist institution has not changed today.

The widespread nature of Christianity's prejudice can be seen in churches across the nation on any Sunday morning. In most of our churches we pray publicly for the parishioner with cancer, a heart attack, or pneumonia. But rarely will a conservative church publicly pray for Mary with severe depression, Charles with incapacitating panic attacks, or the minister's son with schizophrenia. Such a conspiracy of silence further communicates that these are not acceptable illnesses for Christians to have. And by our silence we further wound those in pain.

Not only do Christians shoot their wounded, but most of the world inflicts injury on those suffering with mental problems. Condemning the emotionally distraught is rampant in our society. A public opinion survey found that 71 percent believed mental illness was due to an emotional weakness; 45 percent said it was the victim's fault—they could will it away if they wanted to; and 35 percent believed it was the consequence of sinful behavior.[6]

Well-publicized examples of such prejudice include the case of Thomas Eagleton, who in 1984 was forced to withdraw as a U.S. vice-presidential candidate because he had once been treated for depression. Similarly, President Reagan made an offhand comment about presidential candidate Michael Dukakis's treatment for depression, apparently hoping to discredit Dukakis's ability to be president. Fortunately, that comment didn't go very far in the press. On the other hand, the media had a heyday with Kitty Dukakis later.

Even the medical and psychological fields are not immune from this problem. A Forum on Stigma sponsored by the U.S. Department of Health and Human Services found that even health care professionals harbor unconscious, unstated negative feelings about their mental patients.[7]

In a recent medical journal, a physician wrote the following:

If you are sick and disabled, it must be in some way because you want to be. . . . The sick have enough misery from their illnesses. Should they now have to put up with the burden of their physicians and their relatives harboring a subliminal suspicion that it is their fault? . . .

Before we allow ourselves the liberty of accepting that the sick somehow deserve what they get and letting that subtle judgement somehow intrude into the way we cope and care for patients, let us be absolutely sure we are right. So far, the evidence is not there.[8]

So this is a universal prejudice. Unfortunately, on this issue Christians in general are as biased as the secular world, if not more so.

"Don't Seek Professional Help"

In the preface I describe the philosophy of some missionaries who have severe emotional struggles but "still won't seek professional help." The church as a whole not only criticizes the person with emotional symptoms, but also opposes their seeking help.

Christian author Dave Hunt, whose books have sold over a million copies, says: "The average Christian is not even aware that to consult a psychotherapist is much the same as turning oneself over to the priest of any other rival religion. . . . There is no such thing as a *mental* illness."[9]

This simply is not true. It is one of the most unfortunate ideas ever published. Dave Hunt greatly lacks understanding of emotional illness. His attitude is a classic example of how Christians shoot their wounded— often mortally.

*   *   *

While I was putting the finishing touches on this book, a very successful singles' pastor drove over a hundred miles to see me for a consultation. His father had been incapacitated by depression, and now he was suffering with the same malady. His family physician had prescribed an antidepressant which had proven to be very effective. But this pastor felt condemned and guilty—condemned to the same fate as his father, and guilty because he needed to take medication. Unable to fight off his depression without medicine, he had decided that he should quit the ministry, and he assumed I would encourage such a decision.

During that initial consultation, I was able to share some of the essential truths in this book. They literally set him free. He left the office feeling grateful that someone understood him and his problem, relieved of a tremendous amount of guilt, and assured of hope for his future. My prayer is that this book will give hope to all of you who are hurting. And for those who are not hurting, I trust it will enable you to be an instrument of healing, rather than wounding, to those around you.

In this book I will share (in lay terms) some recent scientific documentation that mental illness is as real as diabetes, cancer or heart disease, and that it often can be treated very effectively. But first let's look at why we wound those already hurting.

— 2 —
Why We Wound

N OT LONG AGO A COLLEAGUE WROTE TO ME ABOUT ONE OF HIS PATIENTS,
Marge, who had to be hospitalized:

> She was comatose and unable to control her bodily functions as a
> result of severe depression. Her pastor . . . had told her, "Snap out of
> this. Our people are getting tired of praying for you!" She [later] said,
> "God knows I would have if I could have; I didn't want to feel that
> way."[1]

Why do we so often hurt those who are wounded among us? One reason
may be that we fail to comprehend the complexity and severe pain of
emotional suffering.

"Like a Branding Iron in the Pit of My Stomach"
More than a decade ago I suffered with severe depression. A patient for
whom I cared very much had committed suicide. Medically, I had done
everything possible for him: I had obtained the necessary consultations,
had used the appropriate medications, and had hospitalized him. Yet,

with his death, I felt I was a failure and couldn't shake the intense feelings of inadequacy. I knew that losing a patient through suicide was an occupational hazard—the average psychiatrist loses one patient every eight years—but the knowledge did not help.[2]

For over three months a devastating sense of doom kept me feeling desperate and hopeless. It felt like a branding iron in the pit of my stomach, twenty-four hours a day. There was no relief. Though exhausted at night, I would lie awake in bed with that suffocating anguish. When I finally nodded off, a fitful sleep came only for a couple of hours. Then I'd awaken, distressed, only to lapse into another restless sleep. Long before dawn I'd be up again, feeling "wired," unable to sleep yet more exhausted than when I went to bed.

This agonizing pain hovered over me like a black cloud and affected virtually every aspect of my mind and body. Normally I enjoy food and need to limit myself so that I don't gain weight; but during those dreadful months, food repulsed me. I literally had to force myself to eat—as I knew it was necessary—yet I still lost many pounds.

Fortunately, I am gifted with strong determination and willpower. So to get some relief for my depression, I applied all the constructive principles I knew and had taught my patients—principles that had helped many of them to cope. Yet the overwhelming feelings of despair continued, and I felt trapped. I forced myself to socialize, exercise and think on positive things; I spent additional time in the Word and in prayer. But I couldn't—by willpower alone—shake the depression. It took every ounce of energy, determination and commitment to God to keep me from taking my own life.

What an irony—that I, a practicing psychiatrist, should find myself in such a dreadful predicament. For a long time I felt that with God's help I "should" be able to lick this problem. But the symptoms persisted. Finally, reluctantly, I sought the assistance of a colleague.

It's hard to know why this was helpful. I suspect that several factors were at work. Admitting my dire need for another person's help, being able to be totally honest and open with someone whom I respected and still feeling that person's acceptance, and getting objective feedback without judgment or criticism—all these things were important elements in lifting the depression.

I hope my experience gives us a glimpse of the magnitude of emotional pain felt by the truly depressed person, and helps us to see the trite solutions given by some Christians for what they are. An article in an outstanding Christian magazine stated the following as the primary solution for fighting depression: "First of all, we can refuse to take [depression] too seriously."[3]

As stated earlier, all too often Christians fall far short in comprehending the depths of these difficulties. Can a person with an IQ of 150 understand what life is like for one with an IQ of 75? Or can a healthy person really appreciate how difficult it is for the quadriplegic to get through a day? Yet these handicaps are much easier to visualize and appreciate than the afflictions of those who suffer with devastating obsessions, phobias, anxiety or depression. Recent studies of more than 11,000 individuals have verified that depression is more physically and socially disabling than arthritis, diabetes, lung disease, chronic back problems, hypertension and gastrointestinal illnesses. The only medical problem found to be more disabling than depression was advanced coronary heart disease.[4] No wonder a senior certified public accountant and a dedicated Christian—whom no one would suspect has a care in the world—recently told me that he would rather have the most severe, disabling physical illness he could imagine than his chronic depression.

The U.S. Department of Health and Human Services reports that individuals who have suffered both emotional illness and cancer report that their emotional illness caused them the greater pain. In addition, the obstacles faced by recovering patients after treatment for their illnesses are often as difficult to overcome as the illness itself.[5]

In *When Life Isn't Fair*, my daughter, Susan, and I wrote about her life-and-death struggle with leukemia.[6] In a two-year period she endured eight hospitalizations averaging a little over a month each. Chemotherapy and total body radiation reduced her blood counts to almost zero and kept her in isolation for weeks at a time. She had fevers as high as

105 degrees, terrifying drug reactions, and nausea and vomiting which made it almost impossible for her to eat a bite of food. In spite of the aggressive therapy, the leukemia recurred, and she was told there was no possibility of a cure. She was expected to live only a few weeks or, at best, a few months. But God allowed for a miraculous father-to-daughter bone-marrow transplant, and she has remained completely free of any sign of leukemia for nine years now.

Eighteen months after the successful transplant, Susan felt physically well enough to resume her preparation for a teaching career. However, while doing her student teaching, she found the overall circumstances and dilemmas of trying to teach three different high-school English classes—one with severe discipline problems—an overwhelming task. She became anxious, depressed, and emotionally and mentally paralyzed. In her opinion, the crippling of her mind and will in this experience was far more painful to her than the physical trauma of the leukemia. "The leukemia could only hurt my *body,*" she said. "In fact, the hardest parts of the battle with the leukemia were the uncertainty and fear, the loss of control, and the drug reactions. But the emotional paralysis I felt while student teaching—that affected my mind and my will! That threatened *who I am as a person!*"

Abraham Lincoln once wrote, "I am now the most miserable man living. If what I feel were equally distributed to the whole human family, there would not be one cheerful face on earth. Whether I shall ever be better, I cannot tell; I awfully forebode I [will] not. To remain as I am is impossible. I must die or be better, it appears to me."[7] Those of you who have or are experiencing severe emotional pain know firsthand what Lincoln and I are talking about. I trust that those who are emotionally healthy can begin to comprehend the plight of those going through deep emotional suffering.

It's tempting for people with everyday stress and its accompanying anxiety or depression to think that those with severe emotional problems feel much the same as they do, only a little worse. After all, they think, isn't depression merely feeling "blue" or "down," and anxiety just plain worry or nervousness? The answer is an emphatic "No!"

Imagine the excruciating pain of a construction worker whose legs have been crushed by tons of concrete. Now visualize the mild discomfort of one with an ingrown toenail. Can you see how hard it is for a person with an ingrown toenail to grasp the intensity of the pain of crushed legs?

One minister writing on depression states that he was depressed for several days after a property contract had failed. As I read through his book, I had the distinct feeling he hadn't experienced the deep depression with which I'm familiar, but only a pain of ingrown-toenail proportions. No wonder he writes, "As a basic rule I never sympathize with depressed people. . . . These people have already pitied themselves excessively, thus generating their depression. What they need is help, which comes by gently getting them to see that they are indulging in self-pity."[8]

His "basic rule" is a totally inadequate solution for a very complex problem. Deep depression is not just self-pity. And those who think so completely miss the scope, magnitude, and multiple factors leading to depression. Many Christians who speak or write on emotional symptoms such as depression, anxiety, phobias, or obsessive thoughts don't have the faintest idea how enormous these infirmities can be. They really don't know what they are talking about.

For some a graph can vividly illustrate my point. (If you don't like graphs, feel free to skip to the following section.) Figure 1a illustrates the mood swings of an emotionally healthy person. Bar 1 represents his feelings on a very good day; bar 2 depicts his mood on the most terrible day he can imagine—such as when he's failed a comprehensive exam necessary to graduate from college. Now compare this with the exhilaration of a very happy occasion—the bride and groom on their wedding day (bar 3)—and an occasion that takes one to the depths of grief—the death of a child or a spouse of forty years (bar 4). The feelings of these "normal" people, however, don't begin to compare with the pain of those diagnosed with emotional illness.

In figure 1b you can begin to see the degree of pain suffered by those with "normal" emotional stresses (bars 1-4) as compared to a typical day

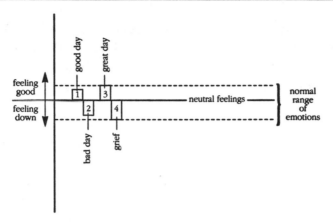

Figure 1a. The feelings of a "normal" person

in the life of those with serious emotional problems (bars 5-8). The pain of burnout (bar 5), which causes the most moderate clinical depression, is a little more severe than "normal" grief. Compare this with the level of distress of the person with moderate clinical depression, also known as dysthymia (bar 6), major depression (bar 7) or manic-depressive illness (bar 8). I will define these illnesses later, but for now I simply want to show how much more intense is the pain of these disorders (experienced

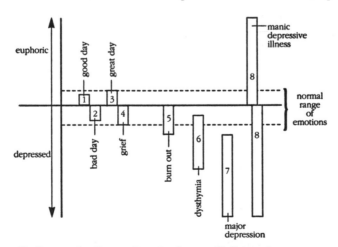

Figure 1b. Comparing "normal" and "abnormal" depression

by up to 25 percent of the American population) than the pain of "normal" depression (experienced by about 75 percent of the population).

Notice that the individual with moderate clinical depression (dysthymia) feels pain even on his best days. He never has a "good" day. The one with a major depression feels much worse, even at his best, than does the "burned-out" individual. The feelings of one with a manic-depressive illness can be ecstatically high one day and swing to a deep depression a few days later.

Figure 2a illustrates different levels of anxiety. A higher line means greater anxiety. The horizontal axis shows the intensity of anxiety over a twenty-four-hour period. Normal anxiety, such as clashing with a difficult boss or worrying over a teenager who takes the car for the first time, is shown as a small blip.

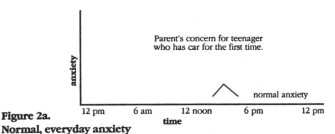

Figure 2a.
Normal, everyday anxiety

In contrast, figure 2b shows the level of anxiety of those with both generalized anxiety and panic attacks. Such people have significant anxiety levels even during sleep. The ever-present emotional pain fuels their fear that the anxiety will never go away. They are afraid they will

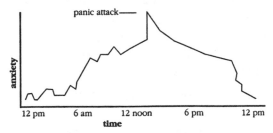

Figure 2b.
Generalized anxiety and panic attacks

lose their jobs, make fools of themselves, "go crazy" and be locked up in a mental hospital or even commit suicide.

Imagine you are being held hostage on an airplane that has been hijacked by terrorists. You have witnessed the brutal murder of one passenger, and you hear the terrorists threatening to kill all the others, one by one. How do you feel? Now imagine living with this level of anxiety every day, and perhaps you can begin to identify with the person who suffers from extreme anxiety.

"I Feel Bad, No Good, Defective!"

Another kind of pain, seldom appreciated except by those who suffer with it, is the deep-core feeling of shame. One of my patients described it this way: "I feel bad, no good, defective." Some say they feel only nothingness or emptiness; others describe themselves as worthless or unlovable. A forty-five-year-old pastor's wife feels so worthless that she usually stands in a corner of my office with her back toward me as she relates how badly she feels. Patiently and compassionately I try to assure her that God accepts her and that I accept her, and she struggles to believe me.

A minister put it this way: "I serve and serve—but I don't have anything in me. I feel so ashamed. I hate myself." On another day he agonized, "I am what I do. Without doing, I feel worthless; and even when doing my best, I feel worthless."

The other morning I saw four patients, three of whom described their despair and hopelessness. They had a deep conviction that they didn't deserve to exist. They believe they are permanently flawed. These three women are all committed Christians who know the "correct" theology on this subject. Some even teach it. Although they believe intellectually that God loves and values them, the trauma of their early years blocks any penetration of this truth into their innermost being. That no one seems to take their pain seriously only intensifies their sense of worthlessness and shame. Last week a new patient, a Sunday-school teacher, sighed and told me, "I am so relieved—at last someone understands what I am feeling."

Telling these women to read the Bible more, to pray more, to think or act right, is not enough. In fact, it can often make them worse.

"Just Get Busy for the Lord"

We often attempt to solve the problems of those with emotional illnesses by urging them to "get busy for the Lord." But pressing the immature and the wounded into service is like sending the soldier whose leg has been blown off back to the front lines.

Try putting a five-year-old who hasn't learned to read into a seventh-grade class and expecting him to learn like everyone else. Whether he stayed in that class for one or twenty years, he would still perform poorly, and he'd act and feel extremely dense and pitifully slow. Believe it or not, we deal with people this way in the Christian community. We expect human beings to go from sinners to saints overnight, regardless of their innate abilities or handicaps. True, our *position* before God is that of a saint, but we must still live and deal with present emotional pain or past trauma. By laying the heavy load of service on these silent sufferers, we often wound them more. The burden of our expectations can actually delay—sometimes indefinitely—the time when they can effectively use their energies in God's work.

Counselors: Priests of a Rival Religion?

Not only do Christians grossly underestimate the severity and complexity of people's emotional pain, but they also frequently communicate a mistrust of the professional counselor. This is the second reason that Christians hurt the wounded. The "Dave Hunts" in our midst view us, in his words, as "priests of a rival religion." Currently I am listening to a series of tapes by a professor of a local Christian university. He makes a number of disparaging remarks about mental health professionals. Not only do many Christians have strong prejudices against emotional difficulties, but they hold an even greater bias against professional counseling. Some Christian writers believe that all counselors, even those who are dedicated Christians, have been "seduced" by the secular philosophy of this field.[9]

A patient of mine, whom I'll call Burt, was asking me some questions about his depression and the criticism that he often felt from the Christian community. I thought this manuscript might clarify some things for him, so I offered him a copy. Just as I was handing it to him, I remembered that he has attended Grace Community Church, pastored by John MacArthur, for a number of years. I hesitated and told him that he might want to pass on reading the manuscript, since in it I make some critical remarks about MacArthur. He emphatically said he would like to read it anyway.

A month later he returned, saying he appreciated and learned a lot from the manuscript. Curious about his reaction to my comments about his pastor, I asked, "Was I too hard on him? Should I soften that part?"

"Oh, no," he said; "I attend John MacArthur's church because I really like his expository preaching—but he doesn't understand emotional illness. Whenever he preaches on this subject, whether it's about the existence of emotional illness or the need to see a therapist, it's really hard for me. There is no way I would ever tell a person at Grace Community Church that I am seeing a psychiatrist or taking medications."

Not that there isn't plenty to criticize about psychology. Yes, the field has been influenced by some who propagate a narcissistic, humanistic philosophy. Many therapists are antagonistic to Christianity. There are even "Christian" therapists that I would not recommend and some "Christian" books on the subject that I have strong reservations about. But how unfortunate and unfair that trained, dedicated therapists who are both Christians and professionals are judged guilty by association. Meanwhile, throngs of hurting people in the church are limping along, avoiding the help they desperately need, and often getting worse in the process. Few of these Christians would avoid seeing a medical doctor or a dentist because he obtained his training from a secular university. Why do they feel that secular training brands Christian counselors as heretics?

If we apply the same guilty-by-association reasoning to other professions, much of our knowledge and progress in society would have to be discarded. In throwing out those who learn from non-Christians, virtually all who help us in one capacity or another would have to be excluded.

Certainly we would have to exclude all who keep up-to-date with scientific advances. Even many ministers take courses from secular schools during their career. Within certain limits, we can learn much from non-Christians. We are encouraged to take advantage of the knowledge available to us as long as it doesn't conflict with the Word of God.

God sent Moses to the educational center of an ungodly world, Egypt, for his first forty years of training. Daniel and Joseph probably received a major portion of their education from teachers antagonistic to Jehovah God. Nevertheless, God used these men as instruments for the deliverance of his chosen people.

*　　*　　*

As you reflect on this chapter, maybe you identify with Marge, the accountant, the pastor's wife, the minister, or the Sunday-school teacher. Perhaps you have personally felt the pain of being "shot," even though you are wounded already.

On the other hand, maybe you have never struggled with serious emotional problems, but you have friends or relatives who do. You have often wondered if their problem is sin, or whether something else is causing their difficulties. Let me assure you—most definitely—that they cannot be simply written off as sinners. Nor can they get better merely by buckling down and reading their Bible. The fact remains that some Christians have circulated a lot of misguided, twisted thinking about what the Scriptures teach on this subject. I will tell you more about this in chapter three.

— 3 —

Can a Spirit-Filled Christian Have Emotional Problems?

I HAVE ALREADY MENTIONED MY DAUGHTER'S BATTLE WITH LEUKEMIA. AT that time she had done everything she could do, both spiritually and medically, to conquer this cancer. She was so ill from the chemotherapy that she couldn't even read her favorite comic strip, *Garfield*. While she lay in the hospital, she received this letter:

Dear Susan,

You do not know me personally, but I have seen you in church many times. . . .

I have interceded on your behalf and *I know that the Lord is going to heal you if you just let Him.*

Do not let Satan steal your life—do not let religious tradition rob you of what Jesus did on the cross—by His stripes we were healed.

I have done what the Lord instructed me to do, but I cannot make you read these [books on healing]; only you can do that.

Be whole, Susan—spirit, soul and body.

In His love,

[Name withheld; italics mine][1]

Is it any wonder that for several months this letter created tremendous inner turmoil? The writer meant well, but failed to be helpful. The theology behind this letter appeared on a bumper sticker I saw recently: "Health and Prosperity: Your Divine Right." Many in the Christian broadcast media preach this "health and wealth" gospel, which states that if you are walking in the Spirit, you will always have a sound body and be prosperous. By implication this "gospel" includes emotional health. The converse is also emphasized: if you are not prosperous and not physically healthy (or, by implication, emotionally healthy), then you are not walking in the Spirit. A segment of Christianity accepts the "health and wealth" precept without question; others don't subscribe to it. But almost everyone subconsciously endorses what I call an "emotional health gospel." That is, if you have no sin, pray right, and read God's Word, you *should not* have an emotional illness; you will have a sound mind free of any emotional symptoms. In short, this "gospel" says, if you are a Spirit-filled Christian you should not have emotional problems. Though many Christians oppose the "health and wealth" gospel, they fail to realize that they still hold to an insidious variation of this "gospel." Recently I was shocked to hear a well-known evangelical speaker take this position. She said: "At the cross you can be made whole. Isaiah said that 'through his stripes we are healed' . . . not of the physical suffering, which one day we will experience; we are healed of *emotional* and *spiritual suffering* at the cross of Jesus Christ" (italics mine). In other words, a victorious Christian should be free of any emotional distress. Another variation of this message is "Christ is all you need."

Isn't Christ All You Need?
The spouse of one of my patients called me and questioned my weekly sessions with his wife. "After all, isn't Christ all she needs?" he said. He had just finished reading John MacArthur's book *Our Sufficiency In Christ: Three Deadly Influences That Undermine Your Spiritual Life*. His thesis is as follows:

As Christians, we find complete sufficiency in Christ and His provisions for our needs. There's no such thing as an incomplete or deficient

Christian. Our Savior's divine power has granted to us everything pertaining to life and godliness. Human wisdom offers nothing to augment that. . . .

So to possess the Lord Jesus Christ is to have every spiritual resource. All strength, wisdom, comfort, joy, peace, meaning, value, purpose, hope, and fulfillment in life now and forever is bound up in Him. Christianity is an all-sufficient relationship with an all-sufficient Christ.[2]

A large portion of the book strongly criticizes psychotherapy as one of the "deadly influences that undermine your spiritual life." Yet I agree with a number of points in his book, such as the statement that some "Christian therapists" have indeed wandered a long way from the Scriptures and the sufficiency of Christ. In his chapter "Does God Need a Psychiatrist?" he correctly acknowledges that "there may also be certain types of emotional illnesses where root causes are organic and where medication might be needed." But he incorrectly goes on to say that "these are relatively rare problems."[3] As I will show you in chapters four and five, they are *not* rare problems.

I would also take issue with the way he *applies* the truth that Christ is sufficient for every aspect of life. I know some individuals will surely "shoot" me for my convictions about the correct application of the Scriptures (2 Tim 2:15), so let me give a few examples.

Most people consider it appropriate to call a roofer when the roof leaks, a plumber when the sink won't drain, or a tow truck when a car won't start. Though God could miraculously solve each of these problems, in most instances he doesn't. It has nothing to do with his ability or his sufficiency for the task. He is able to, but he chooses not to use that means. Rather, his sufficiency enables me to deal with these problems and get whatever help is needed to solve them. There is no question that God is *ultimately* sufficient.

Let's take a closer look at Christ's sufficiency in a temporal medical problem. Consider the person with a club foot. Sixty years ago many people born with a club foot struggled with this handicap for their entire life. Fifty years ago I remember seeing other children on the streets with this deformity. Their playmates made fun of them. Their activities and occupations were limited. For such a handicapped Christian, was Christ sufficient? Yes—but we have to define "sufficient." For the most part Christ did not remove the disability in a miraculous way, just as he did not remove Paul's "thorn in the flesh." Instead, God said to Paul, "My grace is sufficient for you, for power is perfected in weakness" (2 Cor 12:9). Paul's response was, "Most gladly, therefore, I will rather boast about my weaknesses, that the power of Christ may dwell in me." In other words, Paul experienced God's sufficiency not by having him remove the weakness, but by being able to handle the weakness or deficiency in an appropriate manner and by seeing more clearly that it was God who worked through him and in him.

Now let's return to the example of the person with a club foot. Fifty years ago—and in a lot of underdeveloped countries today—God shows his sufficiency by giving the grace to handle the deformity in a thoroughly Christian manner. With the advances of medical science, it is certainly appropriate today for Christians and non-Christians alike to obtain the expertise of an orthopedic surgeon. It neither opposes God's will nor denies the sufficiency of Christ to have an operation to correct the abnormality.

I suspect that those of you who concur with MacArthur's position would agree that seeking the services of a plumber or a surgeon is not denying the sufficiency of Christ. But I also suspect that you will feel uncomfortable with the direction I am heading with this illustration. In chapters four and five I will show conclusively that physical illnesses affect all organs of the body—including the brain and its functions. And one of the brain's functions is our emotions. Though it is much more difficult to recognize and accept, many imbalances—more subtle but just as physical—can affect our emotions. God doesn't need a psychiatrist, but some of his saints do.

MacArthur's views illustrate a fuzziness in much of Christendom about the differences between the physical, emotional and spiritual spheres of influence on one's mind. For example, he refers to "so called Christian psychologists and psychiatrists who testified that the Bible alone does not contain sufficient help to meet people's deepest personal and emotional needs." He then concludes, "These men were actually arguing before a secular court that God's Word is not an adequate resource for counseling people about their spiritual problems!" Note in the first instance he speaks of emotional needs and in the second about spiritual problems. On another page he discusses psychology and its treatment, but then switches and says that "psychotherapy cannot solve anyone's spiritual problem." True, psychology cannot and never will be able to solve humanity's spiritual problems—only Christ can. But note again the fuzziness between the emotional and spiritual spheres. In yet another place he refers to "deep emotional problems" and then concludes that "those who see therapy as the best means to cure a sick or wounded soul are trying to substitute fleshly devices for the work of the Spirit."[4]

Fuzziness in delineating the cause and nature of an emotional problem will lead to inappropriate solutions. Later in this book I will show that there is a truly *physical* aspect of our brain: it has cells, chemicals, and minute electric waves that, when altered, can cause a significant number of our mental problems. Abnormalities in the physical realm cause a lot more difficulties than most individuals suspect. Certainly they are not rare.

Other mental illnesses have specifically *emotional* causes. This arena includes our many thoughts, memories, past emotional injuries, immature ways of handling emotions, and interpersonal relationships. Any of these elements can contribute to mental disorders. While original sin and another individual's sin certainly play a part in problems with emotional causes, one's own personal, unconfessed sin need not be a factor.

Mental problems can also have *spiritual* causes. In fact, any abnormality or difficulty might have a physical, an emotional or a spiritual root cause. I will elaborate on this later, but for now I will say that I firmly believe the only true solutions for spiritual maladies come from God's Word. While the Bible is truly sufficient for everything in the spiritual realm, it doesn't address all the issues in the physical sphere. Thus appropriate medical or psychiatric care may be God's means of remedying a physical problem. Is God able to miraculously intervene? Absolutely. I have seen that at times he does. But it doesn't necessarily mean he will. One day, however, God will give us our resurrected bodies and all these "weaknesses" will be removed.

In the emotional sphere, portions of Scripture such as the book of Proverbs give us much help. But the Bible is not primarily a book on emotions any more than it is primarily God's revelation on the anatomy of the brain. All truth, including psychological, emotional or biological data, is God's truth whether Holy Writ explicitly elaborates on it or not. And there is a lot of truth the Scriptures do not elaborate on. However, no real truth, regardless of the realm of knowledge, will contradict the Scriptures. The Bible must always remain the "gold standard." *No "truth" outside the Scriptures that pertains to mental disorders should be accepted if it is contrary to God's Word.*

More on this issue later, but for now let me reiterate my original point: a large segment of Christianity believes in an "emotional health gospel." If this "gospel" had been held throughout the ages, its proponents would have written off many outstanding Christian leaders as hopeless sinners. That is what they are doing today, not only to Christian leaders but also to ordinary, struggling Christians.

Saints with Emotional Illnesses?

In my psychiatric practice, I have generally not found that individuals with emotional problems were sinning or being naive Christians. I have a few patients whose problems are truly spiritual—that is, they are deliberately choosing a path contrary to God's Word. In these situations I use Scripture to address the problem. But most of my patients are sincerely trying to follow God's will. I have many patients who are ministers, missionaries, Bible study leaders, elders and deacons. Yet they have emotional problems. They find it encouraging to know they are not alone.

Many saints have struggled with emotional symptoms. Martin Luther, the great leader of the Reformation, influenced millions of individuals for Christ. For centuries he has inspired Christians with his "salvation by grace through faith alone" theme and with hymns such as "A Mighty

Fortress Is Our God." But Luther also experienced periods of serious doubt and emotional distress. In 1527, he wrote the following: "For more than a week I was close to the gates of death and hell. I trembled in all my members. Christ was wholly lost. I was shaken by desperation and blasphemy of God." He found himself "subject to recurrent periods of exaltation and depression of spirit. This oscillation of mood plagued him throughout his life." Luther himself stated that "the content of the depressions was always the same, the loss of faith that God is good and that he is good to me."[5]

Charles Spurgeon was one of the great preachers of all time. He drew ten thousand people to his London church on a Sunday morning; he lit the fires of the nineteenth-century revival movement; and his sermons and books still influence those in ministry the world over. From his *Little Secret Diary* we discover his deep commitment to Christ. At age sixteen he made this entry: "I vow to glory alone in Jesus and His cross, and to spend my life in the extension of His cause, in whatsoever way He pleases." Years later he wrote, "I pray God, if I have a drop of blood in my body which is not His, let it bleed away."

But this same preacher who displayed unwavering commitment to Christ also lived with great emotional turmoil. "From boyhood days dreadful moods of depression repeatedly tormented [him]," one biographer wrote.[6] His despondency forced him to be absent from his pulpit two to three months out of the year. In 1866 he openly shared his struggle with his congregation: "I am the subject of depressions of spirit so fearful that I hope none of you ever get to such extremes of wretchedness as I go [through]."[7] During these depressions, he said, "Every mental and spiritual labor . . . had to be carried on under protest of spirit."[8]

J. B. Phillips has had a far-reaching impact through his books such as *Your God Is Too Small* and *New Testament Christianity* and his translation of the New Testament. He once said, "God has never been known to disappoint the man who is sincerely wanting to co-operate with His own purposes." But on another occasion he said, "It's truly a devastating thing . . . to be ill in your innermost spirit." His dark thoughts and mental pain seemed to lock him in a prison with no key. Irrational fears would grip him at night, unreal guilt swept over him, and his sense of God disappeared. During his worst times, God seemed remote and unapproachable. Phillips called it "the dark night of the soul." His wife indicates that he "had to cope with psychological disturbance and dark depression" for a period of fifty years.[9]

Many prominent Christians have suffered with serious emotional difficulties, especially depression. Most contemporary Christian leaders, with few exceptions, keep their struggles to themselves. But when we continually hide our anxiety or depression, we in effect endorse the "emotional health gospel."

Embracing this "gospel" tends to blind us to the teaching of the Word of God on this subject. The Scriptures tell us that significant negative emotions plagued some of God's chosen deliverers and prophets in the Bible. Moses, Elijah, Job and Jeremiah suffered from depression, often to the point of being suicidal (Num 11; 1 Kings 19; Job 3; Lam 1—5). I don't believe that any sin of theirs caused the deep, painful emotions. Yes, their pain resulted from Adam's original sin and its effect on humankind, as well as the deliberate sin of other human beings. Nevertheless, Moses', Elijah's, Job's and Jeremiah's own deliberate sins did not cause their emotional distress.

We read of David's frequent depressions in many of the Psalms. No doubt his sin with Bathsheba (which he writes about in Psalm 51) caused some of his depression. But at other times his depression seemed to come from stresses such as threats on his life by Saul or Absalom. In Psalm 6 he writes:

I am pining away; . . .

my bones are dismayed.

And my soul is greatly dismayed; . . .

I am weary with my sighing;

Every night I make my bed swim,

I dissolve my couch with my tears.

My eye has wasted away with grief. (vv. 2-3, 6-7)

In Psalm 22 we read:

My God, my God, why hast Thou forsaken me?

Far from my deliverance are the words of my groaning.

O my God, I cry by day, but Thou dost not answer;

And by night, but I have no rest. . . .

My strength is dried up. (vv. 1-2, 15)

Moses, in the midst of the glorious days of leading the children of Israel out of Egypt, became so discouraged that he wanted to die. In Numbers 11 we read how he poured out his heart to God: "Why hast Thou been so hard on Thy servant? And why have I not found favor in Thy sight, that Thou hast laid the burden of all this people on me? . . . So if Thou art going to deal thus with me, please kill me at once" (vv. 11, 15).

Elijah's miraculous victory over the prophets of Baal is recorded in 1 Kings 18. But in the very next chapter we see a different man—despondent and trembling with fear: "He was afraid and arose and ran for his life. . . . and sat down under a juniper tree; and he requested for himself that he might die" (1 Kings 19:3-4). Many Christians today teach that Elijah was a coward. In fact, they accuse Elijah of having a grand old "pity-party." They fail to see God's compassionate response to his cry: "The angel of the Lord came . . . and touched him and said, 'Arise, eat, because the journey is too great for you' " (19:7). The Lord allowed him to rest and twice sent an angel to feed him. Notice the absence of any criticism from God and the tenderness in the way he dealt with his servant.

Jeremiah, "the weeping prophet," clearly obeyed God when he repeatedly warned the idolatrous nations of Israel and Judah about God's impending wrath. After being ridiculed, persecuted, and imprisoned by those he warned, and after seeing the destruction of Jerusalem, his beloved city, Jeremiah wrote Lamentations. Note the depth of his anguish:

Look and see if there is any pain like my pain . . . .

He has made me desolate, . . .

My spirit is greatly troubled; . . .

There is no one to comfort me; . . .

My eyes fail because of tears, . . .

I am the man who has seen affliction . . . .

Even when I cry out and call for help,

He shuts out my prayer. . . .

And my soul has been rejected from peace; . . .

So I say, "My strength has perished,

And so has my hope from the Lord." (Lam 1:12-13, 20-21; 2:11; 3:1, 8, 17-18)

As you read Jeremiah's words, those of you who have gone through deep emotional pain are undoubtedly saying, "This man knows how it feels—I can relate to him." You can also take comfort in knowing that the cause of Jeremiah's depression was not his own personal sin.

In looking at Job, we find that (in God's words) "there is no one like him, . . . a blameless and upright man, fearing God and turning away from evil" (Job 1:8). Yet under stress he became depressed and hopeless. A few passages from the Living Bible graphically illustrate his despair:

Job spoke, and cursed the day of his birth. . . .

Why is a man allowed to be born if God is only going to give him a hopeless life of uselessness and frustration?

I cannot eat for sighing;

My groans pour out like water. . . .

My life flies by—day after hopeless day. . . .

I hate my life. . . .

For God has ground me down, and taken away my family. . . .

But I search in vain, I seek him here, I seek him there, and cannot find him. . . .

My heart is broken. Depression haunts my days.

My weary nights are filled with pain. . . .

All night long I toss and turn, and my garments bind about me. . . .

I cry to you, O God, but you don't answer me. . . .

My heart is troubled and restless. (Job 3:1, 23-24; 7:6, 16; 16:7; 23:8; 30:16-18, 20, 27 LB)

But notice that in spite of Job's honest expression of his depressed feelings to God and to his friends, the Bible says, "Through all this Job did not sin" (1:22). Moreover, God tells Job's friends, who had accused him of some grave sin, "You have not been right in what you have said

about me, as my servant Job was. . . . Go to my servant Job and offer a
burnt offering for yourselves; and my servant Job will pray for you, and
I will accept his prayer on your behalf, and won't destroy you as I should
because of your sin, your failure to speak rightly concerning my servant
Job" (Job 42:7-8 LB).

Scriptural Commands: Clubs or Splints?

Christians often quote specific passages of Scripture that they think will
help people with emotional symptoms. Unfortunately, the recipients of
these pithy passages usually feel like they're being clubbed. One frequently wielded club is the apostle Paul's phrase, "Be anxious for
nothing" (Phil 4:6). What was most likely intended as a word of gentle
encouragement by Paul has been turned into an explicit command that
can be broken, rendering us guilty of sin. If you are anxious for any
reason you are sinning, the thinking goes, so just stop being anxious.

But I find it noteworthy that the same Greek verb for "be anxious"
(merimna) is used earlier in Philippians 2:20, where Paul commends his
coworker Timothy, saying, "I have no one like him, who will *be genuinely anxious* for your welfare" (RSV). The Word Biblical Commentary
says this is a strong verb, which carries "overtones of the pressure or
weight of anxiety that grows out of true concern for the welfare of
others."[10] The same word translated "anxious" in Philippians is used in
2 Corinthians 11:28 to describe Paul's "concern" *(merimna)* for the
churches. This could have been translated just as correctly, "There is the
daily pressure upon me of *anxiety* for all the churches."

A closely related verb is *to fear.* In fact, our word *phobia* comes from
the Greek word *phobos,* which is used many times in the Scriptures.
Many passages, such as Matthew 10:28 ("do not fear those who kill the
body"), tell us not to fear. Nevertheless, Paul indicated that he himself
felt fear: "And I was with you in weakness and in fear and in much
trembling" (1 Cor 2:3). Later he wrote, "Our flesh had no rest, but we
were afflicted on every side; conflicts without, fears within. But God,
who comforts the depressed, comforted us by the coming of Titus" (2
Cor 7:5-6). In fact, we are sometimes even encouraged to have fear:

"Therefore let us fear" (Heb 4:1); "be obedient . . . with fear and trembling" (Eph 6:5); and "work out your salvation with fear and trembling" (Phil 2:12).

Anxiety and fear are important, God-given emotions. There are numerous situations where they serve us well. For instance, some anxiety is necessary to prompt the typical student to study for an exam. Or if your fifteen-year-old and some classmates are driving down the street at one hundred miles per hour, let's hope they feel some anxiety and outright fear.

These Scriptures and examples indicate many times and ways in which feelings of anxiety or fear are not sin and, in fact, may be very constructive. The same is true for anger. Though some biblical passages warn us not to be angry, other sections and examples actually instruct us to be angry, but to handle it without sinning.[11]

If we persist in believing that negative emotions are sinful, we must come to terms with the biblical examples of Christ's emotions. He experienced strong negative feelings in the Garden of Gethsemane: In Mark's words, "He . . . began to be very distressed and troubled. And He said to them, 'My soul is deeply grieved to the point of death' " (Mk 14:33-34). The Amplified Bible renders it more powerfully: Christ was "struck with terror and amazement and deeply troubled and depressed. And He said to them, 'My soul is exceedingly sad—overwhelmed with grief—so that it almost kills Me!' " Jesus, in coming to earth, took upon himself the form of man with all its frailties—including the propensity for negative human emotions—yet did not sin.

I do not question that many negative emotions are a result of Adam's sin and its effect on the human condition. But I am convinced that negative emotions—depression, anxiety, guilt, obsession and any others—are *not necessarily* due to an individual's unconfessed sin.

You see, we are imperfect vessels. We will never be perfect in this life. Accepting this fact takes a big load off of us. As Paul says, "But we have this treasure in earthen vessels, that the surpassing greatness of the power may be of God and not from ourselves" (2 Cor 4:7). We are all earthen vessels—or you might say "cracked pots."

The Greek word *astheneia* means "weakness, infirmity, want of strength or inability to produce results." It does not describe sin, but rather an imperfection or defect. It's the word used in Hebrews 4:15, which says, "For we do not have a high priest who cannot sympathize with our *weaknesses*." When we restate this double negative it reads, "We *do* have a high priest, Jesus Christ, who is able to empathize with our weaknesses." The King James renders *weaknesses* as "the feeling of our infirmities." Hebrews 5:1-3 tells us that the Old Testament high priests were able to help others because they were also "beset with *weakness*." Paul uses the same word in Romans 8:26: "So too the [Holy] Spirit comes to our aid and bears us up in our *weaknesses*" (Amplified). The verse doesn't say he removes the weaknesses, but that he helps us in them.

Thus when we look at a word or feeling such as anxiety, we must see what the entire Word of God has to say about it (Acts 20:27 KJV). One commentator says of Philippians 4:4-6, "The figure of speech called 'asyndeton' runs throughout this section, where commands are given in rapid-fire fashion without any connecting words to link one command to the other."[12] Thus the command in verse 6 to "be anxious for nothing" is a summary statement; we must use other passages to help us understand it and its application in greater detail.

In 1 Corinthians 8 and Romans 14, Paul commands stronger Christians to be sensitive to people with a weaker conscience—often manifested by feelings of anxiety. But he does not come down hard on these individuals. Instead, he says that "we who are strong ought to bear the weaknesses (*astheneia*) of those without strength" (Rom 15:1).

Paul elaborates further in 1 Thessalonians 5:14: "And we urge you, brethren, admonish the unruly, encourage the fainthearted, help the weak, be patient with all men." Here the church is to "admonish the unruly," in other words, warn the incorrigible, undisciplined, or idle with a firm reminder. The church occasionally needs to firmly warn a person, but not usually the needy, hurting individuals with emotional difficulties. Admonishing them would wound them. The next phrase tells us to "encourage the fainthearted." Here the Greek word means "to speak kindly, closely, tenderly to the fainthearted" (*oligops*). This is the only passage where this word appears in the Scriptures, and it literally means "small-souled, feeble-minded, despondent or depressed and discouraged."[13] Other Greek scholars say it could apply "to worry, fear, or discouragement," or to the person who feels "worried," "anxious," "weary," or "defeated."[14] Greek scholar Ernest Best says, "The *worried* are not admonished but *encouraged*. . . . To rebuke them would not deal with the heart of their trouble."[15] The next phrase, "help the weak," encourages the church to support or hold a person who is weak (*astheneia*). We need to offer splints to support their broken bones, not clubs to beat them with!

Christ makes a statement nearly identical to the much-quoted Philippians 4:6 passage. In Matthew 6:31, he says, "Do not be anxious." But then he elaborates on the subject of anxiety and gives us a better understanding of the subject (Mt 6:25—7:5; Lk 12:4-34). He says not to worry about temporal things—what you will eat, drink and wear. He pinpoints the blatantly disobedient, anxious, covetous, materialistic individual with the strong rebuke "You fool!" But others he tenderly encourages to consider his care of all living things and how useless worry actually is. Thus I believe Christ shows empathy to the weak and struggling by encouraging them to trust in him. He says, "Do not be afraid, little flock, for your Father has chosen gladly to give you the kingdom" (Lk 12:32).

When we glibly tell struggling people not to be anxious—though we can literally be right—we may be as blind to the bigger picture as the Pharisees were. By rebuking instead of encouraging and supporting, we may be dead wrong and very wounding in our method of helping. Perhaps that is why the passage in Matthew 6 about worry is immediately followed by a strong exhortation in chapter 7 not to judge one's brother.

While the church should never condone willful sin, it must learn to accept that people within it may suffer from emotional symptoms that do *not* stem from personal unconfessed sin. They may be weighed down with depression, anxiety, obsessions, false guilt or some other disorder, but they need our help and understanding, not our condemnation.

For those still convinced that emotions such as anxiety are always sin, let me propose a little experiment. Give me the most saintly person you know. If I were to administer certain medications of the right dosage such as amphetamine, thyroid hormone or insulin, I could virtually guarantee that I could make this saint anxious with at least one of these agents. Would such chemically induced anxiety be sin? You might respond, "If he or she is dumb enough to take such a drug without needing it, it might be sin." But what if the person's own body had an abnormal amount of thyroid hormone or insulin and produced nervousness—would he be sinning? I have seen patients in this exact predicament. I'll let you judge whether these individuals are sinning.

Bible Reading and Prayer: Pat Answers?

In May 1991, *Moody Monthly* carried a feature article entitled "Christians on the Couch," which addressed the raging battle in Christendom over the use of Christian counseling. In it, John MacArthur stated, "I'm convinced that what we're seeing is one of the most subtle and effective attacks Satan has ever mounted against the church. . . . Bible reading and prayer are commonly belittled [by Christian therapists] as 'pat answers.' . . . This attitude . . . amounts to a 'denial of the faith.' "[16]

In 1964 my brother, Paul, was martyred as a medical missionary in Zaire. Several years later, another physician assumed his responsibilities in the hospital where Paul had worked. With a desperate need for supplies, he wrote to me for help. My response was a well-composed, erudite letter in which I reminded him that God had called him to that work and he would, therefore, "supply all your needs." Then I quoted a Bible verse to support my "encouragement."

On one hand, everything I said was "right" and very scriptural. On the other hand, I was dead wrong in the *way* I used Scripture. I was giving him a pat answer. I was in residency training at that time and my life was extremely busy, so I simply dumped the problem back on him. It would have been far more honest for me to write, "I'm sorry, I sense your great need but I am unable to help at this time. I'll be praying that God will provide someone who can." I didn't have the courage to be that honest. In fact, at the time I thought I *was* giving an honest answer. Only in more recent years—when I began to think about pat answers—did this example come to mind, along with a sickening feeling of remorse. I now know that I gave him platitudes instead of help, and that an honest answer would have been better than my "scriptural one."

Whether we want to admit it or not, the most valid truth in the Scriptures can be misused and become a pat answer. James reminds us how inadequate it is to give only biblical words when a person needs food and clothing (2:14-20).

Prayer, like Scripture reading, is a crucial part of the Christian life. The Bible is replete with commands to pray; we are even told to "pray without ceasing" (1 Thess 5:17). But prayer, even when combined with Bible study, is not to be treated as the total solution to all our problems. On one occasion, Joshua was on his knees in prayer and God commanded him to stop praying and take action (Josh 7:6-13). In other words, if Joshua had continued to pray, he would have been sinning. In that particular case, there were other things he needed to do besides prayer. In the New Testament, the Pharisees were strong advocates of the Word of God and followed its commands to the letter—yet in the process they neglected many weightier matters (Mt 23:23). Even Satan quoted Scripture (Mt 4:1-10), but applied it inappropriately.

Now in one sense it can never be a pat answer to tell someone to "study the Bible and pray." Bible study and prayer are foundational to the Christian's daily life; we all need to do them. Even many who suffer from emotional difficulties need to apply these more. However, there are many other struggling Christians who are already praying and poring over the Scriptures. I have seen people in deep emotional trouble who were spending four or more hours a day in Bible study and prayer. To simply tell them to do more of this is a pat answer—and the wrong answer. I think of a woman who sat crying in my office, questioning everything about herself: "Maybe if I was more spiritual, or if I gave more time to the church, or if I prayed and read my Bible more, I would feel better." I knew this woman well, and in my opinion her need was not lack of spiritual discipline. To tell her so would have been misapplying the truth. It is not a "denial of the faith" to say that a fundamental doctrine can be misused and turned into a pat answer.

Charles Stanley, senior pastor of the thirteen-thousand-member First Baptist Church of Atlanta and former president of the Southern Baptist Convention, has been greatly blessed by God in his ministry. On November 12, 1992, he spoke candidly at a conference of twenty-three hundred Christian therapists from over forty-three different countries. He first thanked individuals in the audience who had been a significant help to him, including his own therapist. Then in a stirring address titled "The Burden of Emotional Baggage," he told of the emotional issues he had brought into the ministry and how they, along with other stresses, had necessitated a year's leave of absence from the pulpit. He said of that time: "I was living as obediently as I knew how. I look back and think, *God, how could I have been so ignorant and so blind to the things that were going on inside of me?* . . . On the inside something wasn't right. I'd get in the prayer room. I fasted, I prayed. I did everything I knew to do, and somehow it just wasn't working." He was scared to look inside. "Up until that time in my life, if you had asked me how to deal with problems I'd say, 'Man, get on your knees and talk to God, get in the Word of God; he'll straighten out any problem you've got.' That was my answer. And so I'm sure that the Lord knew if he was going to use me at all, he had to get me past that very *juvenile answer* to everything."

We Aren't Created Equal

Deeply ingrained in us all is the belief that God created everyone equal. It would seem both unchristian and un-American to believe otherwise. After all, our Declaration of Independence affirms, "We hold these truths to be self-evident, that all men are created equal."

We *are* equally precious as human beings created by God. In addition, we all have equal assets, in some ways. For instance, we each have one life, twenty-four hours in a day and equal opportunity to accept God's gift of eternal life. Jesus' parable in Luke 19:11-27 portrays this equality: the nobleman, representing Christ, gives each servant the same amount of money to invest until he returns.

However, these truths should not be misconstrued to mean that we all have equal capabilities. In another parable about talents, God gives one person five, another two and another only one talent, "each according to his own ability" (Mt 25:14-30). None of us would question that some have an IQ of 150 and others an IQ of 75, even though the difference may not be apparent outwardly. Some have great athletic ability, while others are "klutzy." Both Scripture and experience indisputably teach that we all have differing capabilities.

Though most will concede that we are not equal in some regards, many will still assume that we have equal emotional abilities. It's hard to comprehend, but some people have what I would call an "Emotional Quotient" of 150, others 100, and others with "one talent" in the emotional realm have an "EQ" of 75. Incidentally, I should point out that the person with an "EQ" of 75 may possess average or exceptional gifts in other areas. A few of these persons might even display the equivalent of three or five "talents" in music, art, athletics, intellectual ability or some other skill.

We don't expect an individual with an IQ of 75 to be a doctor, a lawyer or even a soldier for our country. Nor do we expect an amputee to help put a new roof on the church. Yet we usually expect everyone around us to have the same emotional strength.

Many among us were molested as children, were verbally or physically abused while growing up, or have been affected by biological factors. These people are emotionally handicapped. But we often expect them to function as well as those with no emotional disabilities.

Emma is a fifty-eight-year-old widow with a tenth-grade education. She works three days a week doing janitorial work at a local church. Her father was an alcoholic who physically and emotionally abused her. Her mother was depressed and emotionally absent. Her husband also abused her until he died three years ago, forcing Emma to find some means to support herself. Emma has fought chronic depression for as long as she can remember. She became a Christian shortly after she was married—and this change has given her a firm hope for eternity. But it has only partially helped her severe melancholy. She has had some counseling, but the cost limits her access to it. Her family doctor has prescribed antidepressants, which have proved helpful, but not without some troubling side effects. In all of this she tries to be cheerful, and one would never know she lives in a constant melancholy. Emma exemplifies for me an individual with limited innate assets—with a lower than normal EQ—who is doing her best to cope with what she has. God freely and lovingly accepts her just as she is. But do we?

It's Adam's Fault

As already stated, I believe all of humanity's problems are ultimately due to sin; but a great deal of our struggles result from Adam's fall rather than our own individual sins. The effect of original sin penetrates every aspect of our world and our lives. C. S. Lewis has written:

> [God] began to rule the organism in a more external way, not by the laws of spirit, but by those of nature. Thus the organs, no longer governed by man's will, fell under the control of ordinary biochemical laws and suffered whatever the inter-workings of those laws might bring about in the way of pain, senility and death.[17]

A. W. Tozer put it this way:

> The moral shock suffered by us through our mighty break with the high will of heaven has left us all with a permanent trauma affecting every part of our nature. There is disease both in ourselves and in our environment.[18]

We can't blame all our problems on Adam and Eve and original sin; but the basic disease processes were set into motion at that time, and its effects have penetrated every area of our lives.[19]

This disease process has affected not only our physical bodies but our emotions as well. We are just beginning to comprehend the numerous ways our bodies and minds have been affected by our fallen nature.

Lewis L. Judd, former director of the National Institute of Mental Health, claims that "brain sciences are currently growing faster than any other branch of the life sciences." In 1991 he said that in the last ten years we have discovered 90 percent of all we know about the human brain.[20] With the rapid growth of knowledge in this area, in all probability the same statement will be able to be made ten years from now. No wonder President Bush declared 1990 to 2000 the "Decade of the Brain."

The data coming in, I believe, clearly show that emotionally we are not created equal. In the next chapter I want to share some of these facts, which indicate that the basic cause of many emotional problems is biological—or, in lay terms, physical.

PART II

What Causes
Emotional Illness?

Some say it's all in the mind and soul—a deliberate choice to disobey or ignore God and the teachings in his Word. But in recent years, study after study has shown that emotional illness can be traced to biological (physical) causes, or to trauma suffered in early childhood or as recently as last month.

Simple explanations of the cause of emotional illness just don't exist, because we are all fearfully and wonderfully—and differently—made. To say that an emotionally ill person is totally and personally responsible for his or her problem because of personal choices and actions is tantamount to saying that someone with diabetes or heart disease chose to be ill. Personal responsibility plays a part in emotional illness, but in almost every case it is only one piece of the puzzle.

In chapters four, five and six we will look at physical and environmental causes of emotional illness—"nature" and "nurture." Chapter seven will deal with the role of personal responsibility. When we are trying to pinpoint exactly the source of an emotional illness, it is never wise to allow the individual to abdicate personal responsibility. The real answer is never as simple as "my genes—or my parents—are to blame." As we will see, most cases involve a combination of nature, nurture and choice.

— 4 —

It's Not
Necessarily
"All in Your Mind"

ELEVEN YEARS AGO I BEGAN WORKING WITH JERRI, AN ATTRACTIVE WOMAN in her forties who had been emotionally and physically abused as a child. Her symptoms included depression, suicidal tendencies, an urge to bang her head against the wall when she felt unhappy, and repeated negative thoughts about herself. When I first saw her, she said that she intended to kill herself by the time her children reached eighteen.

She started psychotherapy, which helped some. But when her children reached maturity she became quite depressed; fortunately, antidepressants enabled her to get past this difficult time—and stay alive.

Because she felt God had let her down as a teenager—by failing to deliver her from her abusive family—Jerri had no use for him. Despite this, Jerri had a marvelous conversion experience several years ago. Both she and I were very hopeful that this would drastically improve her emotional status. She became involved in a church, joined a meaningful prayer group and endeavored to apply scriptural principles to her life as best as she could. The genuineness of her Christian experience was manifest in dramatic changes in her language and a deep concern that family members would also accept Christ.

But Jerri continued to struggle with many of her original symptoms, though they did not incapacitate her as before. She believed Christ had resolved her eternal destiny, but obsessive thoughts continued playing in her head like a broken record: "You're stupid. You're ugly. You can't do anything right . . ." These messages droned on by the hour and couldn't be driven out even with Bible study and prayer.

Then a new medication for obsessive-compulsive symptoms was released. I recommended that she try it, and reluctantly she did. Several weeks later she returned, thrilled with the results. "I feel like a different person!" she proclaimed. "I'm in a state of shock!" The obsessive, racing thoughts that she had struggled to control were now gone. It utterly amazed her to discover that her mind could be at such rest. Comments that once hurt her so deeply now seemed to bounce off. "All the old garbage is gone," she said. "It's been hell. It had control of me, but now I have some control." For the first time in her life she wanted to live; she felt she had been given a new life. Love, joy and peace had been merely names for feelings she was now experiencing for the first time in her life.

Jerri's story is unusual, but it vividly illustrates the biological nature of some emotional illnesses.

Before we look at how physical many emotional illnesses are, let's look at the incidence of mental illness in society. In the general population, we know that 15 percent have a diagnosable emotional disorder at any one time. A diagnosable emotional illness is defined as one that causes symptoms serious enough to affect one's ability to function. It warrants the person's seeking professional help and meets the clinical criteria of a mental illness as established by the World Health Organization, which classifies all diseases. For an illness to meet such criteria it must be a recurring pattern of behavior that causes significant pain or impairment in the individual's functioning.[1]

At any given time, 15 percent of the population is suffering with a mental disorder. During his or her life span, an individual has a 32.2

percent probability of developing a serious emotional problem. Ten percent of the population will need hospitalization for an emotional illness.[2]

To visualize these statistics, think of a group of one hundred people. At any point, fifteen of them will be struggling with an emotional disorder. If you follow these same one hundred individuals, thirty-two of them will experience a significant emotional problem sometime, and ten will have a psychiatric hospitalization.

Do these statistics also apply to Christians? Until recently we could only speculate on the answer. We would like to think that we are immune to these problems and that the incidence of these illnesses is negligible among our ranks. Studies are beginning to appear in scientific literature that show religious commitment to be only "somewhat" helpful in reducing emotional problems.[3]

In chapter eleven I will elaborate on how faith in Christ can improve one's mental health. In fact, I believe that a proper application of scriptural principles can be *extremely helpful* in decreasing emotional symptoms. However, at this point, I will simply state that the incidence of mental illness in Christians is fairly similar to that of the general population.

Now that we have established that emotional illness is not rare, and that slightly less than 32 percent of Christians will suffer with a significant mental disease during their lifetime, we will address a crucial question: What causes mental illness?

Nurture, Nature or Choice?

Over the centuries, everything from an excess of passions to the malevolent influences of the moon to evil spirits to the gods has been cited as the cause of mental disease. With the development of scientific thought and discoveries, in the seventeenth century the role of physical agents such as germs became apparent; soon illnesses that had physical symptoms and an observable tangible cause were referred to as "physical" illnesses. Those that didn't seem to have a tangible physical cause and affected the emotions were called "mental" illnesses. It seemed logical to assume that such illnesses were caused by poor control of one's emotions or thoughts. They were labeled "emotional" or "mental" illnesses. Over the centuries this distinction has become firmly entrenched in our thinking: that all physical illnesses are caused by some tangible physical alteration and all emotional illnesses are caused by the faulty handling of our emotions. The former lies essentially out of our control; the latter, it is assumed, remains under our control. This dualistic, "either-or," erroneous thinking persists today in the church, in society and to some extent even in the medical community.

But others down through the ages have not been willing to blindly accept such either-or reasoning. For instance, in 1876 Sir Francis Galton, an English scientist, conducted the first studies on twins to try and separate the cause of mental traits; he coined the term "nature and nurture" to distinguish between hereditary and environmental factors. Since then the medical community has argued over whether emotional problems are the result of *nature* or *nurture*—caused by our heredity or our environment. More recently the secular field has emphasized the role of *choice,* something the church has long emphasized.[4]

Let's first turn our attention to the fact that "mental" illness may be due to nature—that is, it may be very physical in origin.

"Rats All over the Ceiling!"

I can vividly remember my first hours as an intern at Orange County General Hospital nearly twenty-nine years ago. "Wet behind the ears," just out of medical school, I felt more than a little trepidation about my responsibility toward the patients. When I arrived on the ward, I heard quite a commotion coming from room 322.

The ruckus came from a thirty-four-year-old man yelling, "Get me out of here—there are spiders and rats all over the ceiling!" He was thrashing about, straining every muscle to free himself, throwing all of his weight against the heavy leather straps that confined him to the bed.

I anxiously asked the head nurse, "Who is he?"

Hardly glancing up from her work, she replied, "Oh, that's Fred—he's been here two days."

"Well, whose patient is he? Can't something be done for him?"

Turning to the roster of patients, she said, "I think he's on *your* list—yes—here he is. He's yours." My heart sank—both for Fred and for myself.

"Couldn't his restraints be loosened? They seem so tight."

"If we do that, he tries to throw his urinal at the varmints he thinks he's seeing. He also tries to pull out his I.V. or jump out the window."

"Ohhhhh," I sighed. "What's his diagnosis?"

"Toxoplasmosis encephalitis."

I mused: a protozoan parasite (or germ) that's hard to treat. I wished—for Fred's and for my sake—that the microscopic infection had attacked his lungs or skin instead of his brain. It could just as easily have done so.

Fred's case illustrates how erroneous it is to think that physical agents affect any part of the body except the brain. We know that numerous bacteria, viruses and fungi can infect various organs of the body. When an organism attacks the liver it's called hepatitis; the kidney, nephritis; the stomach, gastritis; and the heart, myocarditis. In each instance, even though it might be the same organism, the symptoms will vary according to the specific organ it attacks. If the infecting germ attacks the brain or its lining, we call it encephalitis or meningitis.

In genetically caused diseases we notice the same pattern. Some genetic abnormalities harm the pancreas and cause diabetes; others the joints, causing gout. Cystic fibrosis damages the kidneys and lungs; Alzheimer's disease affects the brain. And as we will soon see, many other "emotional" illnesses have genetic causes.

Likewise, hormonal alterations, nutritional deficiencies, errors in metabolism and various physical and chemical agents can selectively affect one or another organ of the body, creating specific symptoms. Each of these can also alter the functioning of the brain, causing an "emotional" illness.

Why make such a big deal of this? Is pinpointing the cause of emotional or mental illness that important? Absolutely. I'm reminded of Hu, a nineteen-year-old Asian immigrant who sought my assistance for depression, anxiety and fatigue. The adjustments he was having to make to an American lifestyle could easily support the theory that stress caused his symptoms. But some subtle physical signs piqued my curiosity, so I decided to check more carefully for a physical or chemical cause of his illness. Somewhat to my surprise, he was suffering from hyperthyroidism—an excess of the thyroid hormone which caused his "emotional" symptoms. With proper medical treatment his symptoms disappeared and he readily adapted to life in the United States. No psychotherapy was needed.

What if I had told Hu that he just needed to read his Bible more and to pray more fervently? I could have quoted Philippians 4:6, telling him that a lack of trust and obedience had made him anxious. I might have thrown in that he needed to quit feeling sorry for himself, or that he should remember that he was much better off than many of his relatives. What if I had engaged him in extensive counseling sessions or put him on mood-altering medications? What a disservice I would have done him.

It is extremely important to know the exact cause of an illness in order to treat it appropriately.

Before I go any further I need to clarify several terms: *biological, organic, physical, chemical* and *genetic*. The words *biological* and *organic* are interchangeable. A biological or organic abnormality involves concrete or structural changes in one's body. In other words, specific anatomical, physical or chemical changes occur. Physical and chemical changes are more particular types of biological changes, and I often use the words *physical* or *chemical* in place of *biological* for variety. *Biological* is the more all-inclusive word used in medicine. Biological problems may be caused by inherited genetic defects, or by nongenetic factors such as physical trauma, a toxic substance, or an infection, for example. All genetic abnormalities cause biological (physical or chemical) changes, but not all biological problems are genetic.

Until quite recently it has been very hard to study the brain in a definitive way. Few people want a biopsy done on their brain or will allow someone to open the cranium to look inside. (Care to volunteer?) As a result, our understanding has lagged fifty to one hundred years behind the scientific investigations of the rest of the body.

For years the only diagnostic tools were X-rays and autopsies, in addition to a lot of armchair speculation. Then electrical brain waves (EEG) and blood flow studies were discovered. Now, sophisticated techniques allow us to study the brain's soft tissue structure and metabolism. In recent years these tools have brought tremendous advances in our knowledge of the brain.

Let's turn our attention to some of the established facts about the origin of a number of specific emotional illnesses.

Pat: Panic and Anxiety

A vivacious twenty-three-year-old secretary, Pat had been extremely healthy until four months ago. While driving across the Los Angeles basin, she blew a tire on a busy but unfamiliar street. When she noticed the graffiti on the walls and people of another ethnic group who seemed to be watching her every move, she grew frightened. Eventually she got help with the car, but the occasion left her with a heightened level of anxiety. Subsequently, whenever she drove more than a few miles from home, dreadful panic attacks ensued. Her heart pounded so hard that she felt it would jump out of her chest; dizziness, shakiness and perspiration overtook her. She feared, she said, that she would run screaming down the street, that she would "go loony tunes" or that she'd die. These attacks came more and more often and began to control her life; then they started to occur in "places that were perfectly safe."

Now, to avoid having a panic attack, she refuses to participate in many activities. For instance, she won't drive more than six miles from home. This kind of fear is called agoraphobia. Such attacks were not uncommon in her family: her maternal grandmother and an aunt had them, and her mother was afraid to ride elevators.

As Pat sat in my office for her first appointment, she asked, "Am I just a 'fraidy cat'? What is the cause of these attacks—physical or mental?"

"To your first question," I answered, "no, you are not 'just a fraidy cat.' I have treated individuals from all walks of life who have suffered with incapacitating panic attacks: Christian workers, an attorney, a physician, a burly contractor and a six-foot-seven, 284-pound professional football player.

"And to your second question—whether these attacks are physical or mental—the answer is *yes*." Across my mind flashed the scientific literature on this illness. First studied in 1869 and called neurasthenia (nervous exhaustion), it proved to run in families. In 1871 it was reported to be common among Civil War soldiers, who called it the "irritable heart." During World War I a major in the U.S. Army encountered many recruits with this disorder and found that 56 percent of them had a family member with similar symptoms.[5] Since then, more sophisticated studies have shown that 7 percent of the population develop panic attacks (with or without agoraphobia) during their lifetime. However, in close relatives (parents, children or siblings) the frequency jumps to nearly 25 percent.[6]

Why does it run in families? Is it due to the environment? Does the mere presence of a family member who has extreme episodes of anxiety make one more prone to repeat this behavior? Or is there some biological or genetic difference in these families that renders them more susceptible to such attacks? How can we tell if the cause is nature or nurture—genes or environment?

To solve this puzzle, researchers reasoned that if they could study twins born into families in which one of the parents had panic attacks, it would shed light on this question. Such reasoning takes advantage of the fact that identical twins have exactly the same genes, whereas fraternal twins have only about one-half of the same genes. However, both identical and fraternal twins have the same environment. If environmental influence is the main cause, one would expect fraternal twins to be affected as often as identical twins. If the major cause is genetic, one would expect the illness to occur in both identical twins but not necessarily both fraternal twins. When many sets of twins with panic attacks were studied, they found that if one identical twin had panic attacks, the second one was five times more likely to have the disorder than the fraternal twin of someone who suffered such attacks. Thus it is now exceedingly clear that genetic factors render certain individuals more vulnerable to developing panic attacks.[7]

How might this happen? The first evidence shedding light on this part of the puzzle came in 1946. It was observed that patients with panic attacks often have an intolerance to overexercising—that is, their anxiety symptoms grew much worse with strenuous exercise. During exercise the body normally produces the chemical sodium lactate. But the sodium lactate level in these patients was much higher than in those who didn't suffer from panic disorders. In addition, these patients had higher blood pressure, glucose and cortisol levels. Then in 1967, Ferris Pitts of the Washington University School of Medicine injected sodium lactate intravenously into individuals prone to panic. He discovered that the injection usually brought on a panic attack remarkably similar to the patients' "worst attacks." A typical patient's comment was as follows: "Have palpitations, tightness—lump in throat, trouble breathing, shuddering sensation all over, can't stop shaking feeling, hard to focus my eyes and things are blurred. I'm very apprehensive and jumpy, this all began with this experiment."[8]

Individuals who were not subject to panic disorders in the first place did not develop attacks when given the sodium lactate. There seemed to be a chemical difference in the individuals who experienced the panic attacks.[9]

A later discovery showed that if patients with panic attacks were given certain medications, such as an antidepressant or a benzodiazapine tranquilizer, it greatly decreased or prevented panic attacks from developing when the sodium lactate was later injected. But most significantly, these same medications blocked spontaneous panic attacks and the internal metabolic changes in patients with panic attacks. These are the medications we now use to help individuals such as Pat.[10]

Further evidence that these patients have chemical differences shows up vividly in their reactions to caffeine. When a dosage of caffeine equal to four to five cups of coffee is given to these individuals, in most cases it triggers a panic attack. Those without a history of panic do not have an attack. Other chemicals yield similar results.[11]

Doctors have also found that telling their patients to relax in order to relieve their anxiety usually does not work. In fact, in six out of ten patients, trying to relax will actually bring on a panic attack! Furthermore, half of all panic disorder patients experience attacks that jolt them out of a deep sleep, sometimes with a pounding heart and shortness of breath. These attacks are unrelated to dreaming; they occur when the person is going from a lighter to a deeper stage of sleep. For some people, "sleep panic attacks" predominate; the same medications help them as those used for awake panic attacks.[12]

All this evidence strongly suggests that these anxiety attacks are not caused by wrong thinking or choice alone, but by underlying biological or chemical factors. The question facing the medical community isn't whether these attacks are due to a biochemical abnormality, but rather the *exact nature* of the biochemical disorder. In simple terms, the latest research shows that in anxiety disorders, the nerve endings "overfire" and excite the brain with chemicals called catecholamines. Medications we use to treat anxiety help reduce this overfiring to a normal level.

So maybe now you can see why I answered "yes" to Pat's question about whether the cause of her panic attacks was mental or physical. It is a mental illness, but it is also very physical—biological, chemical and genetic.[13]

I am not saying that all anxiety is genetic in origin. Nor am I saying that if a family member has such symptoms, one is doomed to have a similar problem. But I am trying to clarify that many people with these difficulties have a clear biological vulnerability to them. Such an understanding can help us be less judgmental and more helpful to the suffering among us.

Closely related to panic attacks are other types of anxieties and phobias. And genetic factors contribute in at least 30 percent of these cases.[14]

Claudia: Obsessions and Compulsions

An average, ordinary, middle-aged woman, Claudia's most noticeable trait is that she is late for almost everything. She won't give you the reason, but if you ask her husband he'll readily tell you why. He would say that everything in Claudia's life requires a horrendous ritual. It takes her two hours to leave the house in the morning. The bed must be made just so. She flosses and brushes her teeth three minutes, then fears that she missed some area and must repeat the task many more times. No dirty clothes can be left in the hamper—they must go into the washing machine so they won't smell up the house. Just to lock the house takes twenty minutes: each window must be checked and rechecked to be sure it's locked, all faucets examined for leaks, the stove and heater inspected at least a half-dozen times. Claudia describes her own behavior as "crazy," but despite her best intentions, she seems unable to alter it.

Claudia has obsessive-compulsive disorder (OCD), another type of anxiety disease which causes recurring thoughts or behaviors. Some have referred to it as a "hiccup of the brain." The constant, senseless, intrusive thoughts must be acted out in rituals to relieve anxiety. Some of these people fret for hours at a time over dirt, fire, germs or death. Others, like Claudia, endlessly check everything. In another case, a man drives around the block every time he hits a bump in the road just to be sure he didn't run over someone. The variations are unlimited. Jerri, whom I described at the beginning of this chapter, also has OCD.

These people know their obsessive thoughts and resulting compulsive acts make no sense, but they can't seem to stop the behavior lest their fear and anxiety overwhelm them. Ten years ago obsessive-compulsive disorder was considered to be a rare psychological illness with no biological basis and a poor prognosis. In the last few years all of that has changed.

Obsessions and compulsions were first described in medieval times, when Latin terms such as *obsessio, compulsio, impulsio* and *scrupulus* were adopted by the European medical community to deal with OCD symptoms.[15] In one early-fifteenth-century example, a priest suffering with compulsions was brought by his Bohemian father for relief. His problem was a loss of reason whenever he tried to contemplate holy thoughts or to visit sacred places. Any time he passed a church he was compelled to genuflect and then thrust his tongue as far out of his mouth as he could. He couldn't seem to help himself.[16]

Fascinating detective work has been done during the last century to elucidate the true nature of this and related diseases. One of the first individuals to look scientifically at this problem was George Gilles de la Tourette, a French neurologist. He described the first case studies in 1885. He noted obsessive-compulsive symptoms in certain people who had movement tics and periodic outbursts of profanity for no reason. This illness is now called Tourette's disorder. One third of these individuals have obsessions or compulsions and many have a family member with obsessive-compulsive disorder.

There are other illnesses besides OCD, such as sleeping sickness or St. Vitus' dance (Sydenham's chorea), which have neurologic manifestations, often obsessions or compulsions, and also show damage to a special portion of the brain called the basal ganglia.[17] Furthermore, in some people with epileptic seizures that originate in the basal ganglia region of the brain, obsessive-compulsive symptoms can appear.

What do these illnesses have in common? Some run in families and may well be genetic. Others are clearly the result of an infection. Sometimes an injury can bring on seizures. But in each instance obsessive-compulsive symptoms appear, as well as an abnormality in a particular portion of the brain. Furthermore, in the past when individuals had incapacitating OCD symptoms and doctors performed lobotomies, the surgery would interrupt the nerve connections in this same basal ganglia region of the brain and would reduce the patients' symptoms.

Recently Lewis Baxter and his colleagues at UCLA have vividly displayed the area of abnormality with multicolored positron emission tomography (PET) scans. In these studies a form of glucose is "tagged" with a minute amount of radioactive material. A computerized scan then shows the amount of glucose processed in each part of the brain. This new technique has verified the area of the abnormality in the brain. In each of the illnesses described above that include obsessive-compulsive symptoms, the scans show an abnormal overactivity in the basal ganglia and adjacent areas.[18] Furthermore, patients with OCD and abnormal scans have normal PET scans after treatment with new medications now available for this disorder.[19]

In the past, most individuals with OCD seemed to hide their disease. It seemed sort of "crazy" to them, and doctors neither understood it nor could treat it very well. Howard Hughes is a well-known twentieth-century example. His lifelong preoccupation with dirt and germs led him to numerous ritualized precautions and to his hermitlike existence.[20]

However, with the breakthrough in medications that have effectively treated 60 to 70 percent of the patients with this disorder, publicity followed and other victims came out of the woodwork. As a result, more recent figures show that 2 to 3 percent of the population will develop OCD during their lifetime. Close relatives have a 20 to 25 percent probability of developing the disorder; another 15 percent will have symptoms but not enough to meet the clinical criteria for the illness. If one identical twin has the illness, studies show a 75 percent likelihood that the second twin will also have the disorder.[21] These findings suggest a genetic basis underlying OCD.

Tourette's disorder also seems to have strong genetic influences. The second identical twin has about a 60 percent probability of developing it, as compared to only a 10 percent probability for the second fraternal twin.[22] Recently some striking results were observed in a set of Swedish triplets. Two months after birth, each baby was adopted by separate parents and raised entirely by his adoptive family. Though they had no contact with each other until age forty-seven, each had developed Tourette's disorder. The role of genetics in this distressing illness cannot be missed.[23]

As our knowledge of these illnesses grows, we seem to be discovering a constellation of disorders that may be "second cousins" of OCD. One strange example that occurs in 2 percent of the population is trichotillomania—the compulsive pulling out of one's own hair. Another example has been described for centuries as "religious scrupulosity." These are not just overly conscientious, deeply devout religious people; by definition their behavior goes far beyond the teachings of their religious groups. For example, one woman feared her soul would be damned because of her sexual thoughts, so she prayed four hours every day about this concern. The medications we use in OCD usually treat both trichotillomania and religious scrupulosity effectively as well.[24] Interesting, isn't it?

To summarize: Severe obsessions or compulsions are often due to a biological abnormality of the brain related to genetic, infectious and possibly other factors. They are not "all in your mind"; they are very physical.

*   *   *

I hope that by now you are starting to see the overwhelming evidence that mental illness is often very physical. Furthermore, the statistics in this and the next chapter conclusively show that organic problems are not "relatively rare"—as some Christian leaders would suggest—but in fact are quite common. In no way does this detract from the sufficiency of Christ or the Scriptures. It only broadens our understanding of human nature and the effects of Adam's fall.

In the next chapter I will verify the physical basis for a few more "emotional" illnesses and then draw some conclusions and applications.

— 5 —

It's Not
Necessarily
"All in Your Mind,"
Continued

IN CHAPTER ONE I TOLD YOU ABOUT SKIP, THE MINISTER'S SON WHO EXPERI-enced hallucinations, delusions and paranoia as a college student. He has schizophrenia, a disease that affects 1 percent of the population. People with this illness suffer from a distorted perception of reality, such as severe auditory or visual hallucinations. One person might "hear" radio signals from an airplane overhead, transmitted directly to her head, telling her she is going to be killed. Another may "see" a nonexistent group of people about to attack him. The schizophrenic's behavior can vary from aggressive and combative to withdrawn and reclusive.

Such major mental disorders have been recognized since antiquity, and usually the victims have been blamed for their illnesses. In the 1950s the in-vogue explanation that an overbearing mother caused the prob-lem heaped tremendous guilt on many unfortunate women, who were dubbed "schizophrenogenic mothers." We now know how wrong this opinion was. As with many other mental illnesses, the origin of schizo-phrenia is primarily biological.

Actually, the first concrete indication that schizophrenia was caused by a physical abnormality came in 1927. When two doctors removed some spinal fluid from schizophrenic patients and replaced it with air, X-rays revealed abnormally large ventricles (fluid cavities) in the brain. Since there was some controversy over the validity of these studies, these findings were pushed aside in favor of armchair speculation for the next half century.

With the recent advent of more sophisticated computerized tomographic (CT) scans, the earlier findings were rediscovered.[1] (CT scans are "pictures" obtained by beaming an X-ray through the brain. A computer maps out the density of the beam after it passes through the brain; it then prints out pictures of the brain, fluid areas and skull.) Now, more than a hundred scientific articles by forty researchers verify that schizophrenics have enlarged ventricles and therefore a smaller brain size than normal.

Figure 1a shows the results of a typical magnetic resonance imaging (MRI) of a healthy individual. (These "pictures" are similar to those produced by a CT scan, except that a radio frequency energy source is used.) Figure 1b shows the MRI of a schizophrenic patient. These are cross-sections of the brain. The light, outer border is the skull. Next you will notice the brain. The dark, central area is the ventricle.[2]

Notice that the ventricles in Figure 1b are significantly larger than normal. On the average, schizophrenics have ventricles 67 percent larger than those of normal individuals.[3]

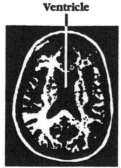 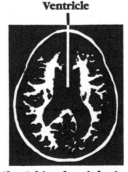

Figure 1a. Normal brain ventricle   **Figure 1b. Schizophrenic brain ventricle**

Anecdotal evidence repeatedly confirms these research findings. Take the case of a seventeen-year-old boy who was admitted to a Washington, D.C., hospital with classic symptoms of schizophrenia. Fifteen months before the onset of any symptoms, the youth was functioning well academically and socially. However, after a minor sports-related injury, a CT scan of his brain found very large ventricles. A completely "physical" abnormality was present at least fifteen months before the onset of his illness.[4] John Hinckley Jr., who shot President Reagan in 1981 and carried a diagnosis of schizophrenia, was found to have enlarged ventricles—after the assassination attempt.[5] Besides the enlarged ventricles in schizophrenics, the section of the brain near the temples is 20 percent smaller than normal, and the number of nerve cells (neurons) is reduced by as much as 44 percent. One study shows a correlation between the decreased temporal brain size and the severity of hallucinations.[6]

In an exhaustive study completed by the department of anatomy and cell biology at UCLA, investigators with powerful microscopes were able to determine the direction that tens of thousands of neurons—individual brain cells—were pointing. They found a visible disorganization of these cells in schizophrenic patients.[7] Figure 2a shows drawings of neurons in their normal pattern, all pointing in one direction. Figure 2b shows the neurons of a schizophrenic patient, all pointing in different directions. Of further interest is that the more disorganized the neurons, the more severe the patient's schizophrenia.

Figure 2a. Normal neuron pattern

Figure 2b. Schizophrenic neuron pattern

Other studies reveal that years before people develop the illness, abnormalities can be noted in their conduct and growth patterns. One researcher concluded: "There's overwhelming evidence that this neurological condition starts in utero."[8]

For years we have known that individuals with schizophrenia were born in the winter and spring more often than in summer or fall. Why? Some postulated that it might be due to viral infections that occur more often at this time of year. To test this hypothesis, a Denmark study reviewed the birth records of schizophrenics covering a forty-year period. The researchers found that mothers who had influenza infections around the sixth month of pregnancy were more likely to have a schizophrenic child. Other studies have verified this finding and have also shown that exposure to measles has a similar effect.[9] We know that rapid changes take place in the child's brain during the second trimester, and a viral infection may account for the numerous physical abnormalities found in the brain of the schizophrenic.

All of these studies drive home the fact that the causes of this illness are not merely an overbearing mother or one's individual choice.

Genetic factors have also been investigated. Parents and siblings of schizophrenics carry, on the average, a 10 percent risk of developing the illness. The child of a schizophrenic mother has a 16 percent likelihood of getting the disease. If both parents have schizophrenia, the probability of having a child with the illness rises to 40 percent. If one fraternal twin has the illness there is a 13 percent probability that the other will develop schizophrenia, but such a probability rises to 50 percent in identical twins.[10]

Classic adoption studies have differentiated further between genetic and environmental influences. If the cause of the illness is purely genetic, then the incidence of a schizophrenic mother's having a schizophrenic child should be the same whether she raised the child or gave it up for adoption into a normal home. On the other hand, if the cause is exclusively environmental, the incidence should be high when the child is raised by a schizophrenic mother and low when he or she is raised by a normal mother.

In a study of schizophrenic mothers who had given their babies for adoption into nonrelated families, the rate of schizophrenia was 16 percent, about the same as for the mothers who raised the child themselves. However, if a schizophrenic mother adopted an infant without any family history of schizophrenia, that child had the same likelihood of developing schizophrenia as the general population—only 1 percent.[11]

Once again, it is clear from such studies that genetic factors can cause schizophrenia. In fact, twin studies strongly suggest that schizophrenia in some groups of patients is as genetically based as diabetes mellitus or hypertension.[12]

It turns out that Eugen Bleuler, the Swiss psychiatrist who coined the term *schizophrenia* in 1911, was right when he argued that it was a "heterogeneous collection of disorders."[13] A recent theory, called the "two-strike" theory, is that schizophrenia is a result of a genetic vulnerability plus an environmental stressor during the second trimester.[14] We can conclude that genetics, viruses and injury can cause or contribute to the development of schizophrenia. In every instance the origin is very biological—or, in nonmedical language, it has "physical" causes.

Mack: Depression

In chapter two I told you about the senior partner of a large accounting firm who would gladly exchange his depression for a "physical illness." His father had had severe depression that required shock treatment, and six years ago Mack's melancholia began to incapacitate him. His "moods" came out of the blue after his company was investigated for some "misleading" financial reports. Though not personally responsible, as a senior partner Mack felt he should have been aware of the problem. He struggled for several years to shake the feelings of melancholia before he came to me and obtained medication that relieved his emotional pain.

Mack is not alone. According to some conservative studies, severe depression affects about 8 percent of the U.S. population at some time during their life. Depending on the severity of the depression and the criteria used to separate between normal and abnormal depression, other studies report a 15, 18 or even 33 percent prevalence.[15]

Depression has multiple causes and can manifest itself in a variety of ways. The mildest clinical form includes the popularized malady called "burnout." Moderate forms generally affect the individual for many years with low to moderate degrees of depression, technically called dysthymia. Very severe clinical depression is called major depression. One type of major depression is manic-depressive illness, which will be covered separately. (See figure 1b in chapter two.)

The scientific understanding of depression probably began with the Spanish histologist Santiago Ramón y Cajal, who is considered the greatest of all neuroanatomists. In 1889 he used a newly invented staining technique and identified the brain cell called a neuron as the primary building block of the nervous system. He also recognized the little tentaclelike structures called dendrites which connect the neurons with each other. Amazingly, he was able to identify the minute area between one neuron's dendrite and the next neuron, which he called the synapse. It is in these infinitesimal gaps that chemicals transmit messages between the brain cells. His work includes an eighteen-hundred-page book containing 887 original illustrations, many of which modern textbooks still reproduce. In 1906 he was honored for his work with the Nobel Prize in Physiology and Medicine.[16]

We now know that the brain has at least fifteen billion of these neurons, each connected at the synapse by chemical neurotransmitters. We can also identify more than twenty different chemical neurotransmitters. In most emotional disorders, these transmitters are altered—there are either too many or too few of these chemicals.

The detective work that has gone into uncovering these neurotransmitters is fascinating. Reserpine, a drug that is an extract from a plant, has been around for centuries. In 1931 it was used effectively to treat hypertension. However, about 10 percent of the patients taking this medication became quite depressed. Doctors learned that it decreased the neurotransmitter norepinephrine. On the other hand, they discovered that imipramine (Tofranil) *enhanced* the neurotransmitter norepinephrine and lifted feelings of depression. It helped not only Reserpine patients but others with depression as well. To this day imipramine still is one of our best medications for treating depression. Facts such as these suggest that the chemical neurotransmitters are the culprits behind many emotional symptoms.[17]

A number of other chemical changes in the bodies of depressed individuals confirm the biological basis of this illness. These include changes in the neuroendocrine system which affect the entire body: appetite, weight, sleep, bowels and sexual drive. Other biological changes in the body can cause depression. For example, in many women the female hormone changes are responsible for their premenstrual depression, a common occurrence clearly related to the menstrual cycle. In one study, 60 percent of women who had significant premenstrual depression later developed a major depression. Postpartum depression—a severe depression that debilitates some women after giving birth—is another example of depression clearly precipitated by endocrine changes in the body. Research has shown that women are more prone to depression than men.[18]

The metabolism in the brain of depressed people is decreased, but it returns to normal levels with antidepressant medication. Also, other studies reveal a 12 percent reduction in the blood flow to the brain in depressed individuals.[19]

Even the lack of light can cause depression in some people. A well-documented form of depression known as seasonal affective disorder usually occurs in the winter. In sunny Florida the incidence of this disorder is 1 percent, whereas in New York it's almost 5 percent. In the long, dark winters of Alaska, 9 percent of residents have severe depression and 28 percent have moderate symptoms of depression. To treat this, one simply has to sit in front of a bright light for a few hours each morning. This phenomenon certainly is "physical."[20]

One might correctly ask, however, whether the biochemical changes in depression are the cause or the effect. Which comes first? Does the chemistry change and cause the depression, or does the depression cause the chemical changes? Particularly in this disorder, evidence indicates that it can start either way. Certainly, some of the time one's environment and choices can precipitate depression which, in turn, effects chemical changes. But in many other situations internal, bodily changes seem to play a primary role.

The fact that relatives of those suffering from depression are more prone to develop the illness also suggests a biological origin. Even the body chemistries of people in these families show similarities. Doctors often find that the specific antidepressant that helped one family member is more effective than other antidepressants for another family member with depression.

Mack, the accountant described earlier, responds beautifully to the exact antidepressant that also helped his father. Periodically I try to reduce the dose of his medication. But when it drops below a certain critical level, Mack changes as though someone flipped on a "depression switch" inside him. The dramatic reaction still amazes me.

In the milder clinical forms of depression, studies sometimes suggest a genetic link, but here the evidence is more debatable. The moderate depression of dysthymia indicates a slightly higher probability of such a connection. In major depression the link becomes clearly evident. If one fraternal twin has major depression, the second one has about a 20 percent probability of having the same. When the twins are identical, the figure jumps to 45 percent—clearly suggesting a genetic vulnerability.[21] More impressive is manic-depressive illness, which we will examine next.

Rolly: Manic-Depressive Illness

During my third year of psychiatry residency at Harbor-UCLA Medical Center, I was assigned to care for Rolly, a musician and composer. Throughout the previous five years his moods had alternated from deep despondence to ecstatic highs—as if he were riding on an emotional roller coaster. The elevated moods charged him with boundless energy, and during these times he slept only one to two hours a night and composed music frenetically. He would spend thousands of dollars to jet across the country to attend a single concert—borrowing money he could never pay back. What initially brought him to our hospital was a disturbance he caused on a flight from New York to Los Angeles. He grew agitated, muttered continuously and threw his dinner tray across the aisle. When the copilot tried to talk to him, he threatened to jump out the door of the plane if "anyone messed with him." He terrified everyone on the flight. The police who were waiting for him when the plane landed in Los Angeles brought him to our emergency room in handcuffs. Hospitalized against his wishes, he had to be physically restrained at times, but medications returned him to a state of normal health so that he could be discharged in three weeks.

However, during the seven months that I saw him as an outpatient, he remained angry at the entire psychiatric profession for hospitalizing and restraining him when his behavior was uncontrollable. He had no comprehension of how sick he was or how seriously he could have hurt himself or others.

Manic-depressive illness, also known as bipolar disorder, manifests itself by extremely wide fluctuations of mood. In the extreme high or manic phase, these patients' endless energy makes them destructively active. When they feel mildly "up," however, they can be very creative and productive. In fact, some of the most creative people have manic-depressive illness (or another type of depression).[22]

In the depressive phase, these patients often "crash" into a suicidal depression. At either extreme, up or down, a psychosis with hallucinations may occur, distorting their sense of reality.

Manic-depressive illness has been around as long as history has been recorded. In the fourth century B.C., Hippocrates proposed the diagnosis of both mania and melancholia.[23] But in spite of its long history, little progress was made in understanding and treating this disorder until several decades ago. Patients with the full-blown syndrome used to spend much of their lives in and out of psychiatric hospitals. Now most of them can function extremely well with medication.

Since leaving my residency training, I have not cared for anyone with as flagrant a problem as Rolly, but I have treated patients with milder forms of this illness. Marty, for example, had everything a person could desire during his four years at a Big Ten university. He was handsome, well-liked and "All American" in his sport. As a Christian he anticipated a great future. Then, one year after graduation, he encountered his first major depression. For the first time, he felt insecure, listless and emotionally paralyzed. From the early morning hours on, an inconceivable fear bombarded him and destroyed all positive feelings throughout the day.

It took an incredible effort for Marty to get up in the mornings, go to work, play with his young children or even go to church. He wanted to hide from the world for fear of being discovered as a real "sicko."

Interspersed with the next twelve years of depression were cyclical periods of great highs, lasting one to three months at a time. Not understanding what was happening to him, he sought professional assistance, but since the biological basis of his illness wasn't appreciated, his agony continued for years.

He was afraid of discussing his "problem" with friends, because he believed it was a symptom of sin. He prayed, struggled, asked God to forgive him and looked for what God might be teaching him. Prayer and confession seemed to be the only answers he heard from conference speakers and church leaders; he wondered if demons caused his affliction.

Finally, he found the help of a psychiatrist who diagnosed his problem as a physical one. He had a bipolar disorder and was started on lithium, a new medication at the time. The results produced an emotional stability that has lasted to this day—twelve years so far.

Now fifty-two, Marty continues to take his medication and functions very well. He remains a dedicated Christian, very active in his church and involved in discipling a number of young men. But because of the stigma, only his wife and psychiatrist know of his "mental illness." He now says, "How I lasted all those years [before seeking professional help] without doing irreparable damage to my person or my career, only a gracious God knows."

What causes this illness? Janice Egeland has been working on an imaginative landmark study on bipolar disorder for more than thirty years. Her team has been evaluating an "old-order Amish" clan in a Pennsylvania community. These ultraconservative Protestants, known for their horse-and-buggy transportation and spartan lifestyle, view a mental illness as the worst ailment afflicting humankind. However, one extended family with bipolar disorder has been found among them.

Egeland's research on this family has yielded much helpful information.

The incidence of bipolar disorder (manic-depressive illness) among the entire Amish community in which the family lives (about 12,500 people) is comparable to the U.S. national average: slightly over 1 percent. But in this one clan of 236 people spanning four generations, 71 percent have experienced major depression—and many have manic-depressive illness. The researchers have identified an abnormality in chromosome 11 of many family members. Further, by examining old family records, the research team traced the illness three more generations back to a patriarch in Europe born in 1763. Though such information doesn't conclusively prove that the problem is genetic rather than environmental, in this instance the evidence suggests a genetic cause.[24]

A number of other studies point to a genetic origin of bipolar disorder. They show that while close relatives and the second fraternal twin have a 15 percent probability of acquiring the disease, the second *identical* twin has a 75 percent chance of acquiring it.[25]

Allan: Alcoholism

Allan, a closet drinker, is one of the 6 to 10 percent of the U.S. population who are alcohol-dependent. He attends church regularly, ushers and helps the needy with miscellaneous chores. Everyone enjoys having him around. No one at church would ever suspect that he touches a drop of alcohol. Even his wife does not know how much he has stashed away in secret places around the house. People at church would be shocked to hear that Allan can be abusive to his wife, or that he may lose his job because he calls in "sick" so often.

Since antiquity, people have known that alcoholism runs in families. In the fourth century B.C. the Greek philosopher Aristotle declared that drunken women "bring forth children like themselves."[26] In the eighteenth century Benjamin Rush, founder of the American Psychiatric Association and one of the men who signed the Declaration of Independence, stated that "drunkenness resembles certain hereditary, family and contagious diseases" in etiology.[27] The first systematic studies of alcoholics, however, were not initiated until late in the nineteenth century. Of all the disorders discussed so far, probably none has generated controversy over its cause more than alcoholism. Is it a disease in which the individual has no responsibility for his actions? Or does it result simply from sinful choices? Scientific research is now giving us solid answers to this question.

One interesting survey of Asians showed that half of them had an unusual enzyme that breaks down alcohol slowly. Because of this enzyme, these Asians are more sensitive to the effects of alcohol and therefore less prone to drink or become alcoholic. The average Caucasian, lacking this enzyme, is less aware of the effects of the alcohol and somewhat more prone to become an alcoholic. At the other end of the spectrum, alcohol-prone individuals have a different enzyme. They are less sensitive to alcohol's effects and so drink more, not realizing the consequences.

Alcoholism has a variety of causes. In the last two decades, however, a growing stack of evidence shows that genetics plays a much greater role than previously known. Allan, for instance, has numerous relatives who are alcoholic. Family studies of alcoholism, regardless of the country of origin, show higher rates of alcoholism among the relatives of alcoholics than in the general population—just as Aristotle observed centuries earlier. Close relatives of an alcoholic are three to four times more likely to have alcoholism than the general population. If one fraternal twin is alcoholic, the other twin has a 28 percent likelihood of having the disorder, whereas an identical twin has a 58 percent chance.

Adoption studies show that the child of an alcoholic parent who was separated from the parent at birth still runs three times the risk of developing alcoholism as compared to persons born to nonalcoholic parents. On the other hand, a child of nonalcoholic parents adopted into a home where one parent was alcoholic has the same likelihood of developing alcoholism as the general population.[28] In summing up this kind of information, a Harvard Medical School expert says, "There is incontrovertible evidence that heredity exercises a significant influence in the predisposition for alcoholism."[29]

On the other hand, not every alcoholic has a genetic predisposition. More detailed investigation shows that some alcoholics do have a genetic vulnerability and others don't.[30] Moreover, even those who do have a biological weakness in this area do not need to yield to the temptation. Though it can be a disease, the individual still has a responsibility for his actions. More will be said about the role of personal responsibility later in the book.

Tom, Dick and Harry: Other Illnesses

Note that the list of illnesses we have just covered includes virtually all the major mental illnesses. That is, almost every major category of emotional illness has at least some biological basis for its disease. Genetics also contribute to disorders such as obesity, anorexia nervosa, bulimia and psychosomatic disorders.[31]

Pervasive developmental disorders in children, especially autism, clearly can be caused by either viral infections or genetic influences.[32] Attention-deficit hyperactivity disorder (also known as ADD, ADHD or "hyperactivity") probably has several biologic causes, one of which is genetic.[33] And this is not an exhaustive list; biological or genetic factors play a role in many other emotional illnesses.

So far I have focused on examples in which someone gets the same illness as a relative.[34] But another dimension of study has noticed that persons with an ill relative may be more prone to other diseases as well. For instance, one-third of ADD patients also met criteria for clinical depression, and family members showed an increase in major depression, anxiety disorders and antisocial disorders.[35] Other family members of a person with anorexia nervosa are more prone to depression or chemical abuse problems.[36] Bulimia shows a relationship to depression, anxiety, phobia, OCD, alcoholism and chemical abuse.[37] Similarly, the families of individuals with anxiety or panic attacks have an increase of depression.[38] Children of parents with depression, anxiety or alcoholism are more likely to have not only similar disorders but also other types of emotional difficulties.[39] Again, this isn't an all-inclusive list, but it shows the crossover from one disease to another in susceptible families.

Increasing evidence suggests that many emotional illnesses may be caused by a combination of several abnormal genes. Depending on the exact combination of genes, vulnerability to a particular disease may manifest itself. This situation exactly parallels that of a number of "physical" diseases such as hypertension, heart disease, diabetes and obesity, to name a few. In other words, a combination of three to five genetic abnormalities gives rise to the weakness to develop the disease, whether it affects our body in general or specifically our mind.[40]

We are fortunate if we don't have to struggle with the illnesses that Skip, Rolly or Allan must contend with daily. But we are, in fact, all "Tom, Dick and Harrys"—or else "Dawn, Vickie and Sherrys." Our biology and genes do affect us in one way or another. It has been said that each one of us has at least four to seven defective genes, though the weakness may never manifest itself. In more minor ways, though, our genes affect every area of our lives—every day.[41]

Even our temperament seems to be determined largely at birth. In the New York Longitudinal Study, investigators found that infants could be categorized into temperament types within the first few weeks of life, and these remained consistent into adulthood! In this study, 11 percent of the babies that were considered "difficult children" turned out to be difficult to raise and had more emotional problems later in life.[42] One leading authority stated, "There are consistent data in the literature to show that genetic factors account for some 50% of the variation in personality trait[s] of neuroticism."[43]

A landmark undertaking known as "the Minnesota Study," headed by psychologist Thomas Bouchard, evaluated more than one hundred sets of identical twins from around the world who were reared apart from each other. They verified that 50 percent of personality and temperament differences and 70 percent of IQ variations were genetically determined.[44] A *Los Angeles Times* science writer captured a fascinating aspect of this research:

> The study has been widely profiled in the news media because of the eerie similarities that have been observed in reunited twins.
>
> Jerry Levey and Mark Newman, for example, were twins who did not meet until the age of 30. When they were reunited, both had similar mustaches and hairstyles, aviator glasses, big belt buckles and

big key rings. Each was a volunteer fire fighter and made his living installing safety equipment. Each drank Budweiser and crushed the cans when he finished.

Levey and Newman are the rule, not the exception, Bouchard has found.[45]

Bonding between the infant and parent very early in life is clearly important for the ultimate well-being of the child. Typically, we blame the mother in cases of poor bonding. However, new studies suggest that the baby's inborn temperament plays a larger role than ever imagined in influencing how the mother reacts to the baby. This temperament and reaction, in turn, help determine the nature of the maternal attachment. When I work with people who suffer as adults because of the lack of a nurturing relationship during infancy, I sometimes get the picture of a little prickly porcupine desperately wanting to be cuddled.[46]

I think of Melissa, a twenty-six-year-old woman who came to me complaining of problems in her relationships. Underneath it all I perceived that no one had ever nurtured Melissa. We uncovered tremendous anger toward her mother for failing to be there for her, although the mother was always available for Melda, her sister two years younger. Then Melissa started expressing these angry feelings to her mother. Ultimately her mother asked if she could come in for a few sessions with Melissa; with Melissa's permission, the three of us met together. Though Melissa's mother had her faults, the primary problem seemed to be that Melissa was an independent child from birth: she "never" wanted to be held, cuddled or placed on someone's lap. So adults tended to leave her alone. When Melda came along and basked in others' affections, it added insult to injury for Melissa. In part, Melissa didn't get the bonding and nurturing she so desperately needed because her temperament was more like a porcupine than a teddy bear.

With so much "physical" evidence accumulating, it's no wonder that genetic studies are moving along at such a rapid pace. At the latest International Workshop on Human Gene Mapping, 139 mental disorders with a known genetic basis were presented. In thirty-six of these disorders, a specific gene has been identified.[47]

The Verdict Is In

The evidence for a biological basis of some emotional illnesses has grown so great that to consider them as different from physical illnesses can no longer be justified. The scientific community is beginning to view these illnesses as having a biological origin. Their validity is even being proven in our courts. For instance, in 1989 a class-action suit was filed in Illinois against two of the largest insurance carriers in that state over payment for manic-depressive illness. The insurance companies did not regard it as a "physical or biological illness." The plaintiff's attorney argued: "The tradition of referring to one group of illnesses as 'physical ailments' and a second group as 'mental illness' arose during an era when medicine was unaware of the physical or biological roots of the latter group. . . . The scientific evidence is [now] overwhelming."[48]

These cases are being won and insurance companies are starting to pay for their treatment just as they would for other medical diseases.

Even state legislators are beginning to enact laws opposing discrimination against mental disorders. For example, legislators in California pointed out that Parkinson's disease, which most insurance companies cover, and schizophrenia, which they usually don't cover, have related problems. In Parkinson's disease there is a deficiency of the neurotransmitter chemical called dopamine; in schizophrenia there is an excess. The author of the bill said, "Medical technology is making daily advances in the research and detection of mental disorders. We need to continually work toward enacting public policy which reflects these advances."[49] The bill was ultimately signed into law by the governor.

Today the following illnesses have the same legal status in many states as any "physical" disease: schizophrenia, schizoaffective disorders, manic-depressive illness, delusional depressions, pervasive developmental disorders and—in at least one state—bulimia, panic disorder and obsessive-compulsive disorder. The number of illnesses is sure to grow, as well as the states and insurance companies recognizing them.[50]

Don't Let Them Get Their Foot in the Door!

Insurance companies oppose giving mental illnesses a physical status because it will cost them too much. Similarly, numerous sincere, Bible-believing Christians refuse to even look at the possibility that an emotional illness could be biologically based.

After I talked about this subject at church, an extremely dedicated, fairly new Christian expressed some criticism. When I heard of his displeasure, I invited him out for lunch. During our lively discussion I discovered his big concern: though there might be some truth to a biological basis for many emotional symptoms, he feared that my speaking and writing about it would allow undesirable individuals and ideas to "get their foot in the door" of the church. In other words, if we give any credence to a biological basis in emotional illness, the Scriptures will lose their position of authority and Christians will rely on psychotherapists to solve their problems. His logic seemed to go like this: Reject everything that secular science says about mental illness to be sure none of this psychotherapy or psychiatry propaganda creeps into the church. It might erode a Christian's confidence in the sufficiency of Christ.

Many feel as this sincere man does. It's much easier for many Christians to view emotional symptoms as "all in one's mind"—under one's control—without an organic basis. Even secular researchers recognize the phenomenon:

> Some believe that accepting a genetic or other biological predisposition to psychopathology is tantamount to accepting a hopelessness about treating or preventing the disorder. . . . Finally, some who resist the importance of genetic and other biological contributions to psychopathology and psychiatric disorders do so because of philosophical and/or religious beliefs. These individuals fear that recognition of the biological basis for behavior and mental function in humans will destroy the basis for "free will" and undermine religious faith.[51]

To the reader who says "amen" to such a statement and considers this book dangerous, I suggest the following considerations.

First, I hope that as Christians we want to know the truth. Through the centuries Christians have often opposed new scientific advances. Yet the truth has never contradicted the Scriptures. Moreover, I believe all truth, regardless of the immediate source, is God's truth. And from Jesus we know that the truth sets us free (Jn 8:32).

Second, biological or genetic factors are never 100 percent the cause of any of the illnesses described above. Our genes are not omnipotent. A secular psychologist, Thomas Bouchard, cautions us: "Just because something's genetically influenced doesn't mean it's chiseled in stone. . . . If I see a child who has problems with aggression, I don't curse genetics. I recommend [assistance for the child.]"[52] Even when our biology or genetics contribute to our problems, we are not doomed by them. Choices are always available to us to minimize the problem. Later in the book I will elaborate on the other determining factors and on the importance of choice.

Third, the more we understand the cause of a disorder, the more accurately we can remedy it. In some instances, this means that Christians will be able to help those who are suffering with greater understanding and compassion. In other instances, such understanding should lead to appropriate professional help—which in no way needs to conflict with a person's walk with Christ. In fact, such help can enhance that walk.

Recognizing biological or genetic influences can free patients, their families and the church from the tremendous blame and stigma associated with these illnesses that greatly compounds their problems. The church will have come a long way when it can view people with genetically based emotional problems as no more responsible for the illness than if they had a heart attack, cancer or Down syndrome.

I do not believe that accepting the biological factors in emotional illness detracts one iota from the sufficiency of Christ—no more than accepting the biological basis of gout or cystic fibrosis undermines one's faith.

*   *   *

The medical community, insurance companies and legislators are all starting to recognize the biological contribution to mental illnesses. My concern and prayer is that Christians in particular recognize these truths and, in the process, extend more grace, compassion and assistance to the wounded among us.

— 6 —

How Childhood
Experiences
and Stress
Cause Emotional
Illness

Six-YEAR-OLD DAVID ROTHENBERG, SEEN ON TELEVISION BY MUCH OF AMER-
ica, was set on fire by his father. The child sustained third-degree burns
over 90 percent of his body, which required more than a hundred skin
grafts. We couldn't help but ache for David as we watched him tour
Disneyland and appear on TV talk shows. It's easy to see and imagine
the physical and emotional scars this boy will have to contend with the
rest of his life.

But the sad truth is, millions of people with perfect bodies are just as
scarred emotionally as David is physically. They suffered physical,
sexual, emotional and sometimes even religious abuse while growing
up. They lacked the necessary nurturing environment so essential to
healthy emotional development; instead they experienced injury and
abandonment.

In 1976 twenty-five youngsters were kidnapped at gunpoint from their Chowchilla, California, school bus. They were driven around in two blackened vans for eleven hours and then buried alive for sixteen hours in a truck trailer covered with dirt. Ultimately, two of the kidnapped boys dug the group out. The three kidnappers inflicted no physical abuse—at least not like David Rothenberg's. But are there scars? Definitely. Years later, Dr. Lenore Terr spent more than a year interviewing these children and their families and found that every child had serious emotional scars. Each one felt significant measures of anxiety, depression, fear, shame and pessimism.[1]

Scarred Physically

The worst physical abuse I ever witnessed occurred while I was working in an emergency room as a resident physician. A very placid six-month-old infant was brought in with an ice pick through his skull. It went in above one ear and came out just above the other. The baby's father had stabbed him in a rage because he wouldn't stop crying. I don't know if the child lived—he was rushed to the neurosurgeons—but if he did, one can only imagine the injuries he sustained.

These examples—a burned boy, a group of kidnapped children and this infant—represent the extreme horrors of abuse. But are there people with whom you rub shoulders each day—family, friends or acquaintances—with scars such as these? Unfortunately, the answer is yes.

Take Bob, a forty-nine-year-old man who seems to lead a normal, orderly life. He is active in his local church, holds a sound theology and genuinely desires to please God. But his emotions and relationships are far from healthy. He has tremendous problems with authority figures in church and at work; he needs to be in control everywhere, especially in his marriage. All of his difficulties can be traced to an abusive father, who locked him out of the house at age two and sometimes tied him to his bed or to the back porch. If Bob did not finish his chores quickly enough, his father whipped him with a three-inch leather belt. He sometimes used the buckle end, raising big welts on Bob's frail body. If he tried to explain himself, he was accused of "talking back" and repeatedly slapped in the face. Then, if he cried, his father warned him that he "would give him something to really cry about." The emotional injury inflicted on him still affects every one of Bob's relationships.

I have counseled many people who have suffered comparable abuse. I can assure you of the reality of their scars and the terrible difficulty of overcoming such deep wounds.

Scarred Sexually

A forty-three-year-old mother of three, Dixie came to see me because she had great difficulty getting to sleep at night: every little noise would startle her and keep her awake in a state of terror. Through the course of therapy she began to remember the terror she had felt every night between the ages of five and eight as she was going to bed. Then gradually she recalled that her father had molested her repeatedly during this period of time. He would come into the bedroom at night to "play," as he put it. She now understands why going to sleep is so hard and why every noise startles her. (Let me point out that more than 50 percent of people who have been molested go through a period of time when they "forget" the molestation.)

Another patient wakes up with terrifying nightmares of the molestation she suffered fifty years ago. Many of these sexually abused find it hard to relate to others and to God in healthy ways because of the cruel mistreatment other people gave them. Humanly speaking, it's exceedingly difficult for these people to perceive God as a loving heavenly Father when their own earthly fathers exhibited such perverted behavior.

Studies indicate that one out of four women was molested while growing up, and one out of six men. Especially in earlier years of this century, such victims suffered in silence over their emotional wounds. They were afraid to tell anyone and were blamed or punished if they did so.[2]

Scarred Emotionally

As a kid I learned the saying, "Sticks and stones will break my bones but words will never hurt me." I believed this was true until I became a psychiatrist and saw the profound destruction done to children with words.

Jill, for instance, was never physically or sexually abused. However, at age four she was told, "If you are bad and don't behave, Mother will leave—and then you'll be sorry!" When Jill began school the next year she was so afraid that "Mommy won't be home after school" that she developed a school phobia. Then her mother said she was "crazy" to feel that way. Further, her mother often berated her by saying, "You're a dummy, stupid and ugly; you'll never amount to anything." When she was nine, her mother got angry at her and said, "I wish I had aborted you in a toilet." Is it any wonder that at age twenty-nine Jill continually struggles with the feeling that she is a "no-good dummy who won't amount to anything," who will be abandoned if she does anything wrong?

Scarred Religiously

Another type of emotional scar is one caused by parents who beat their children into submission with religious clubs. Julie, a very sensitive girl, was often severely punished by her mother, whose harsh words and occasional use of "the rod" would leave her trembling with fear. And then she was told that if she thought this was bad, God's judgment would be a lot worse! Once at age eight, when she said a "bad word," her mother recoiled by saying, "You can't be a Christian and say that!" This statement, to Julie, meant she was going to hell; the condemnation terrified her. To this day—thirty years later—Julie continues to struggle with feelings of worthlessness, fears of being abandoned, and fears of hell. Recently we were trying to figure out why Julie is so terrified as she tries to go to sleep each night. As we talked, several childhood scenes began to emerge. First, she recalled saying the universal children's bedtime prayer every night:

Now I lay me down to sleep,
I pray the Lord my soul to keep,
If I should die before I wake,
I pray the Lord my soul to take.

She never "heard" the last line. Second, at only four years of age, she was forced to listen to fire-and-brimstone preaching illustrated with movies of volcanic eruptions, molten lava and all its destruction. These words and scenes ingrained in her a deep fear that she'd die in her sleep and go to hell. Though she had forgotten why, she always feared going to sleep, even as an adult. All these "religious beatings" made her a compliant and sincere but terrified Christian, until we were able to open the wounds and allow them to drain and heal.

Long-Term Effects

Hundreds of scientific studies now verify the long-lasting and severe nature of various kinds of injuries that can be inflicted on the developing child. Lenore Terr (who worked with the Chowchilla kidnapping victims) draws some parallels between the effects of childhood traumas and the long-term effects of rheumatic fever in children. This disease may produce symptoms when one is young, or it may lie dormant until adulthood. Years after the original infection it can reveal itself for the first time in a variety of ways. Similarly, traumatic childhood experiences may manifest themselves in various ways throughout life: poor school performance, difficulty in trusting others, low self-esteem, hysterical symptoms, psychosomatic illnesses, obnoxious or antisocial behavior, difficulty establishing peer relationships, impulsiveness, violence, overly compliant behavior, eating disorders and the inability to enjoy a healthy sexual relationship.

Many of these symptoms persist throughout one's lifetime, and these people are more prone to major personality disturbances as adults. They may have difficulty coping with anger and aggression, an inability to trust others, lower IQs, a greater tendency to abuse alcohol and drugs, or an increased incidence of depression—including suicide attempts. The unemployment rate is higher for them. And this is by no means an exhaustive list! One report said that every emotional problem studied to date is more severe when there is a history of childhood abuse.[3]

The above list describes the results of abuse in general. Some studies have lumped various types of abuse together—emotional, physical, sexual. Others find it hard to separate the various types of abuse, because most of the individuals have been the victims of multiple episodes of abuse that involve more than one category of exploitation. However, studies specifically relate sexual abuse to drug abuse, criminal behavior, eating disorders, severe personality disorders, multiple personalities, psychosomatic problems, sexual perversion and depression.[4]

For years I have struggled with the passages in Scripture that say the sins of the fathers are passed on to the third and fourth generations (Ex 20:5; 34:7). Now that I have been practicing as a psychiatrist for some years, I see this phenomenon consistently portrayed before my eyes. Without help, the physically and sexually abused children are prone to repeat this pattern of abuse.

Scarred Nurturing

So far I have been describing the effects of flagrant, overt physical and emotional injuries to the developing child and their long-term consequences. But many other kinds of injuries, often more subtle, can be just as damaging.

For instance, in 1942 Rene Spitz published his classic study of 123 infants who had been deprived of maternal nurturing. Each had lost his or her mother during the first six to twelve months of life. All their physical needs were adequately met: they had clean diapers, regular feedings and so on. How did they respond to this treatment? They lost weight, slept fitfully, cried or whimpered a lot, became withdrawn and had more infections than the average infant. In the ninety-one instances where the mother did not return, thirty-one of these children died in infancy.[5]

Early parental loss—through death or permanent separation—causes significant injury. One study of ninety adults who lost a parent between the ages of two and seventeen reported that 71 percent sustained a major psychiatric disorder as adults.[6]

I am convinced that not only the physical loss of a parent but also the emotional absence of a parent can cause significant injuries. Though the effects may not be as dramatic as in Spitz's study, they will be evident in later years.

Almost every day I see individuals who were never complimented while growing up. Their parents believed that if children were praised it would "go to their heads." Even now many of these parents—now typically senior citizens—may praise or compliment their children to others, but never directly to the child.

I know of a man who, in spite of his significant achievements in writing and speaking, cannot recall ever receiving any affirmation from his father. One time, when the father went to hear his son speak at a large meeting, the son asked his father afterward what he thought of the evening. The father meekly said, "I wish I could speak like that!" It was probably the closest thing to a compliment he could say. This situation depicts a father who feels inferior to his son, but it also highlights the lack of nurturing his son received as a child. This deficiency resulted in significant emotional injuries with permanent scars. The man's parents probably raised him the only way they knew how, but he still must deal with the scars.

In addition, injury results when a parent has significant emotional problems. For example, parents suffering with major depression inevitably affect their children. In more than twenty-four studies, 40 to 45 percent of the offspring of parents with emotional problems were found to have some major emotional difficulty later in life.[7]

Current Life Events

You have worked hard all of your life and put all your savings into a bank. Then, due to no fault of your own but to deliberate bank fraud, all your retirement benefits are lost. How would you respond emotionally? How do you think the average person would respond?

In 1985 the First Colonial Bank of the Marshall Islands had to close its doors because of fraud; the perpetrator of the crime, a personal friend of many of the investors, had been employed by the firm for twenty-three years and was president of its credit union. Some 450 investors lost all their hard-earned money. Linda Ganzini and her colleagues studied seventy-two of these investors. Averaging fifty-four years of age, most had recently retired from an electronics firm in the Northwest. Forty-five percent had lost more then $40,000; 14 percent had lost more than $100,000. Within twenty months, 29 percent of those studied showed the classic, severe symptoms of major depression lasting more then six months; one-fourth of these were suicidal. Another 27 percent experienced pathologic generalized anxiety.[8]

These statistics show the dramatic effects of catastrophic events in one's life. I have a number of patients who developed severe emotional symptoms after a significant personal trauma. Several had lost a son or daughter or spouse. Others had missed a promotion or were "let go" from their job. All felt completely shattered.

Other injustices—some caused by our own family—take a tremendous toll on our emotional well-being. Any traumatic event—a loss of something important to us, whether tangible or intangible—can bring on a marked increase in fear, anxiety, depression, psychosomatic symptoms and marital difficulties. These aftereffects may persist for many years.[9] So not only do our early developmental influences play an extremely important part in our emotional well-being, but more recent external factors can also play a role.

Even the Scriptures portray the effect of contemporary life stresses. Though David did nothing to deserve Saul's persecution, he felt tremendous stress when fleeing and hiding for his life, and became depressed. Job experienced depression and wished to die during the testing that was due to his righteousness.[10] Jeremiah, a righteous prophet, suffered horribly because of his obedience to God. His emotional anguish spawned an entire book in the Bible: Lamentations. Paul in 2 Corinthians 4 tells of the extreme stress that circumstances and responsibilities placed on him. If these great men of God suffered from external pressures that caused emotional symptoms, we are certainly not immune.

The well-known "Social Readjustment Rating Scale," developed by Thomas Holmes and Richard Rahe, found a correlation between the changes or stressful events in one's life and the development of illness. For instance, because the death of a spouse causes profound effects, the researchers assigned it 100 points on their scale. The loss of a job merited 47 points. Retirement "scored" 45 points, and in-law troubles 29. In all, this scale lists 43 such items covering most of the traumatic changes in one's life.

Holmes and Rahe found that if a person accumulated more than 150 points in a year, he or she had a 50 percent likelihood of developing a serious illness. Of those with more than 300 points, 90 percent developed a significant illness within the year. Such an illness could be either "physical" or "emotional." This famous study not only demonstrates that stress can cause illness but also shows that the effects of stress are cumulative: they add to each other.[11]

External stresses, furthermore, can contribute to a number of emotional illnesses in susceptible individuals. It has been clearly demonstrated that the following illnesses are often triggered by a stressful life event: schizophrenia, depression, manic-depressive illness, obsessive-compulsive disorder, panic attacks and generalized anxiety disorder.[12]

Sometimes a single traumatic experience plays the primary role in creating problems for us. But more often our problems result from a series of accumulating factors. Take the 56 percent of the investors who developed depression or anxiety following the loss of their life savings. The remaining 44 percent did not develop clinical illnesses. I suspect that those affected had other contributing factors. They may have been victims of childhood trauma or may have had some biological disposition toward depression or anxiety.

In the previous chapter I explained how genetic factors play a role in causing alcoholism. However, environmental factors such as family drinking patterns, behavior problems within the family, the emotional environment in one's growing-up years and the quality of those relationships are all important ingredients that interact with the hereditary factors in causing this disease.[13]

New Creatures, Old Pain

I hope that you are beginning to see that the nurturing received during the early developmental years and the external stresses that come into one's life certainly can cause psychological illness. Yet some Christian leaders such as John MacArthur say, "There is no such thing as a 'psychological problem' unrelated to spiritual or physical causes."[14] Dave Hunt makes a similar statement: "There is no such thing as a *mental* illness; it is either a physical problem in the brain . . . or it is a moral or *spiritual* problem."[15] From the studies I've described in this chapter, you can see that they and a significant segment of Christianity are simply denying the effects of nurturing deprivation, early development and external stress on our psyche.

Over the years I have treated hundreds of beautiful but wounded Christians, people who sought help in their churches but didn't receive any because the wounds of their early development were not appreciated. As I listen to these patients hour after hour, I cannot help but see the deep pain and trauma inflicted on these individuals. Their sincere dedication to Jesus Christ does not always eradicate the ongoing effects of trauma in their lives.

Bob, who was discussed earlier in this chapter, was severely scarred physically and emotionally. Though he seemed to be a dedicated Christian, he had major interpersonal problems. Christian leaders had spent much time with him—to no avail. As I started to probe his areas of deep pain he said to me, "I don't want to talk about my childhood, because 2 Corinthians 5:17 says that I am a new creature in Christ, the old things have passed away and all has become new." Bob accepted Christ at age twenty-one, so his misapplication of this verse eliminated all his formative years from our discussion. He may have read the following passage in *Beyond Seduction:* "For the true Christian the past no longer has any power, but has been done away with through the redemption in Christ's blood. The Scripture says, 'Old things are passed away: behold, all things are become new.' "[16] Shortly thereafter Bob dropped out of therapy, and several years later he got divorced and remarried.

I certainly do believe 2 Corinthians 5:17, but its proper application is crucial. Most of us would not expect David Rothenberg's scars to be miraculously removed through a salvation experience. And we would probably caution the diabetic about throwing away her insulin upon conversion. Why then do we think that deeply rooted emotional scars will miraculously vanish?

*   *   *

How you were treated as a child can provide a solid foundation that helps you to become a well-adjusted adult. On the other hand, it can be a garbage heap of emotional problems that you must dig through every day of your life. If we ignore these childhood influences, we unconsciously allow ourselves to be controlled by the old hurts. We may hide the chaos and dirt from our own eyes, but the odor will still penetrate everything we do.

How you as an individual and the church as a healing community can help will be discussed in chapters nine, ten and eleven. But first let's examine the role of personal choice in these matters.

— 7 —

What About Personal Choice?

W HAT I AM GOING TO SAY IN THIS CHAPTER COULD EASILY BE MISUNDER-
stood and misused, particularly by the very people I am trying to help.
I am going to point out that personal choice does play a part *to some
degree* in emotional illness. Just as people might misuse what I have said
so far by concluding, "My genes made me do it," or "My parents caused
my problems," or "My neurosis is the result of my environment," others
might say after this chapter, "Aha—see, it is *all* choice!"

I hope you will be able to see the need for balancing each of these
ingredients. With that in mind, let's look at four different ways that one's
personal choice can affect one's emotional difficulties.

"It Feels Good"

Ron, a fifty-three-year-old, moderately successful businessman, pro-
fesses to be a Christian and attends a prominent, affluent church. He
came to me complaining that he was not happy. Disgruntled with his
wife of thirty-two years, he said, "She is frigid and bossy, and she pushes

her brand of Christianity on me." Moreover, a relationship had developed between him and his attractive, thirty-six-year-old bookkeeper. "She listens to me," Ron said of her, "and it feels good to be with her."

By our second session the issue seemed clear. I said to Ron:

"It seems that you want me to approve of your relationship with your bookkeeper, yet you also want me to counsel you on the basis of the Scriptures. We both know what the Scriptures say on this subject. I'm curious about something, Ron. You know I am a Christian. If you wanted someone to condone your leaving your wife, why didn't you seek a non-Christian counselor? Why did you choose to see me?"

Ron hesitated, and then replied, "I knew I could get a non-Christian therapist to approve my actions; but I would still feel guilty. I thought if I could get someone like you, a dedicated Christian, to go along with it—then it would be O.K."

"Ron," I said, "I will work with you and support you as a person regardless of what your decision is, but I cannot, as a Christian, condone your leaving your wife. It may well be that your wife has the faults you attribute to her; but since I've never met her, I can only go on your word. My strong recommendation would be for you to break off this relationship with your bookkeeper and for you and your wife to come in together to work on your marriage."

Several days later Ron called and canceled his next appointment, and I've never heard from him since.

As Ron's situation illustrates, sometimes our emotional difficulties arise largely from personal sin. Jonah clearly ran away from God, and no doubt his actions precipitated his suicidal depression. Saul developed psychotic depression as a result of his disobedience to God (1 Sam 15—31). After David's sin of adultery and murder, he became profoundly depressed (Ps 32, 40, 51, 55).

About 80 percent of my patients are Christians who actively seek a Christian therapist and desire to do God's will. Yet I do see people like Ron. Some blatantly lie, cheat the government, have affairs, get drunk, use illicit drugs or want their own way regardless of the effect on others. In such situations my role is to help them see the kinds of choices they are making. These are choices that the Scriptures directly address and that have significant consequences when ignored.

Anger, Grudges and Forgiveness

A closely related category consists of people who are unforgiving. Sometimes their tenacious thirst for vengeance is obvious to all. At other times the grudge can hardly be perceived. Right now, two patients who are struggling to let go of their anger come to mind.

Vic carries around a murderous rage over the accidental fatal shooting of his only son by one of the boy's friends. Vic has vented his rage but can't forgive his son's buddy. I have been trying to help him see the source of his anger: When he was seventeen, Vic's father was killed in a freak construction accident. Prior to this, Vic went to church faithfully and wanted to become a minister; but he hasn't darkened a church door since. Vic still holds God responsible for his father's premature death.

I am trying to help Vic see that his rage is destroying him. At one time he professed to be a Christian, but now he tells me he would go to hell if he died today. Though he needs large doses of medication to combat his severe depression, he probably wouldn't need them if he could give up his bitterness. Fortunately, we can talk very honestly about it. My task with Vic right now is to stay beside him—hoping and praying that one day he will let go of his rage and be reconciled with God.

The longer I stay in this field of medicine, the more I believe that some find it harder to forgive and let go than others. In one study comparing the children of parents with and without manic-depressive illness, researchers observed twelve-month-old babies when their mothers left the room and when they returned sixty seconds later. All the babies cried and fussed when the mother left. But the children with normal parents quickly calmed down when she returned. The children whose parents had manic-depressive illness, however, "held a grudge" when their mothers returned and often stayed angry for several minutes longer if they didn't get what they wanted.[1]

The fact that some people tend to carry a grudge—even at one year of age—doesn't alter God's clear command to forgive. But it does help me understand patients like Vic. It enables me to be more compassionate as we work together to remove the blocks that make forgiveness so difficult for some people.

Naiveté and Poor Models

Personal choice plays a role in emotional health even when poor choices are the result of ignorance, naiveté, poor models or poor instruction. Some people just don't know how to make decisions and need to learn how to make wise choices. Naiveté is not sin. (But if one learns how to choose and then chooses not to apply the new knowledge, it can become sin.) I see many individuals make poor choices because they don't know how, they question their ability or they don't have permission to make better choices.

At thirty-nine, Joanne is an extremely conscientious woman. Her strict Christian upbringing and her legalistic church taught her that having one's own wants and needs was selfish and therefore sinful. After accepting Christ at age eight, she has always wanted to please Christ—but has often struggled with how to do so. She was raised in a small farming community, and the Bible church she attended had only three men her age when she reached adulthood. She did not feel especially attracted to any of them, but on the advice of her minister and parents, she married Frank.

Joanne had always wanted to work in public relations, but she capitulated to her mother's influence that somehow teaching was more Christian. So she taught third grade for several years before having her own children—though she never enjoyed it.

As a wife and mother, Joanne diligently gives herself to her family and to the Lord's work; as a result she never has any time for herself. Her life lacks any fun or enjoyment. Since adolescence she has had a number of physical disorders for which her doctor can find no "physical" basis. More recently, anxiety and depression have taken up residence. She doesn't know who she is or even what she wants to do in life. Without a sense of personal identity, she has become a passive victim of her circumstances and the wishes of those around her.

When Joanne first started seeing me, she desperately needed to gain an awareness of her own feelings, needs and wishes and to realize that it was appropriate for her to take charge of her life within God's will. Initially she got in touch with many negative emotions such as pain, anger, depression and loss. With agony she now realizes that she made lifetime decisions naively. She could have chosen a more desirable career and married a Christian from another church without departing from God's will. She is now changing what she can—taking part-time classes in marketing and enjoying it. Her marriage remains "ho-hum," but she is doing her utmost to make the very best of it—and it's better than it has ever been. She is beginning to appreciate who she is in Christ.

I find it very gratifying to help people like Joanne—to see them mature and become truly free individuals for the first time in their lives—"free indeed," as John 8:36 puts it.

"*Me* Do It"

While working on this chapter, I met with a forty-one-year-old single woman who had been referred to me by her oncologist. She was distraught over the recurrence of her cancer. At the end of the first session I gave her a prescription for a few mild tranquilizers and encouraged her to take them if needed. The next week she appeared just as anxious and unable to cope, so I asked if she had taken the medication. She said she didn't get the prescription filled. "That would be a sign of weakness," she said. "I want to do it myself."

When she wondered whether I understood her feelings, I promptly replied, "I sure do!" I then proceeded to tell her about my daughter's hospitalization for leukemia. Though pain, nausea and fever racked her body, Susan refused all pain medication; she seemed to want to "tough it out" as some sort of challenge. One day a nurse gently rebuked her by saying, "Susan, you don't get any gold stars for not taking pain medicines."

After that session I couldn't help but reflect on how well the Carlson clan has lived out the "me do it" philosophy. As a toddler, Susan would often try to undertake a task beyond her years; if we tried to help, she would say, "*Me* do it."

When I struggled with my depression, I avoided getting any help until I felt fairly convinced that I could not make it on my own. Half of all physicians don't have their own personal physician—and in the past I have been in that camp. When I recently told my wife I had scheduled a routine physical, she cried tears of relief.

I can't remember my father ever going to a doctor when I was young. When he felt too sick to work—which rarely happened—he treated himself with home remedies. I recall the time he misread the label on a bottle of liniment and took six tablespoons—the prescribed amount for a horse—instead of the two teaspoons for a human. More recently, in the midst of a diabetic crisis, my dad refused for several days to go to the hospital. Finally, with all the strength that two ambulance attendants and I could muster, we physically had to force him to go to the emergency room—or he surely would have died. (He's now ninety-two.) I'll let you decide whether these three generations of "independent thinkers" are the result of genetics, environment or Swedish stubbornness!

Back to my main point: Many patients who desperately need emotional assistance or medication have a "me do it" philosophy. This attitude is much more prevalent with emotional problems than with "physical" illnesses. I believe this bias comes because we have bought into the idea that we are 100 percent personally responsible for our emotional illnesses. Many hurting people limp along for months or years, robbing themselves and loved ones of quality lives. Their rationale is: I got myself into this mess, so I need to get myself out (with no external help); otherwise I am weak.

Often those suffering from emotional problems—and their loved ones—need to be willing to get help from those who are able to give it. Accepting help is usually a matter of our will, and often it is pride that keeps us from it.

But the Scriptures provide many examples of people who need to give up their pride to accept help. Doesn't our entire salvation rest upon facing our own inability to be the people we should be and accepting God's help? Naaman had to become willing to wash in the dirty Jordan River—something he didn't want to do—in order to receive God's deliverance from his illness (2 Kings 5). The apostle Paul needed guides to get to Damascus and then required the touch of Ananias to restore his vision (Acts 9:1-19).

Steak or Nothing

One patient, referring to her view of life, told me, "If I can't have steak, I don't want anything." This philosophy essentially means that if I can't have things exactly as I want, then I won't get any help or do anything to make the best of what I have. Some emotional problems are chronic, and a few individuals don't want to do anything to help their condition unless they can be assured of a 100 percent improvement. For them, 80 percent won't do.

Somewhat akin to the "steak or nothing" folks are those who come into my office and want me somehow to wave the magic wand and remove all their problems once and for all, with little or no effort on their part. It seldom works this way. In order for people to find relief from their symptoms, they usually need to do a lot of work.

Even those with severe chronic problems have the choice to do a certain amount to minimize their difficulties. William Glasser is one of the few secular psychiatrists to emphasize the role of personal responsibility in overcoming emotional disorders. In 1962 he applied his principles of Reality Therapy to a ward of 210 chronic schizophrenic patients at the West Los Angeles Veterans Administration Hospital. These poor souls were barely existing; few ever improved or were discharged. Glasser required that the patients start taking some responsibility for their daily care. Although some were only able to feed themselves or brush their teeth, eventually they were able to take on meaningful work, for which they were given extra privileges. Glasser clearly showed that even severely ill psychiatric patients, when given tasks appropriate for their condition, can improve themselves. The program enhanced their self-esteem and allowed many to be discharged.[2]

Martin Luther, whose "whole life was a struggle against [bouts of depression]," did all he could to combat his emotional disorder. In the seventeenth century he discovered many of the same principles that we recommend today for depressed patients. His first rule was to maintain his faith in Christ. He further advised:

> Seek company and discuss some irrelevant matter as, for example, what is going on in Venice. Shun solitude. "Eve got into trouble when she walked in the garden alone. I have my worst temptations when I am by myself." Seek out some Christian brother, some wise counselor. Undergird yourself with the fellowship of the church. Then, too, seek convivial company. . . . Make yourself eat and drink even though food may be very distasteful.[3]

Thus Luther made healthy choices that reduced the effects of his depression.

*   *   *

Whether a problem stems from outright sin, lack of knowledge, or such factors as heredity, biology, development or current environment, we all still possess a degree of control and choice as to how we will handle the situation. We may not be able to eliminate our problem completely—to have steak, so to speak—but we may get ourselves a very good hamburger! I happen to prefer a good hamburger to nothing; and I have often found them better than many steaks. There is often something we can do to better our situation, and even if our action alone does not heal us completely, it is all God expects of us. And it can significantly improve the overall quality of our life.

In later chapters I will elaborate on the steps an individual and the church can take in order to minimize the devastating effects of emotional problems.

— 8 —

Putting It
All Together

REMEMBER THE ILLUSTRATION OF THE BLIND MEN TRYING TO DESCRIBE AN elephant? One grabbed its tail and said an elephant was like a rope. The second man, touching its ear, thought the elephant was like a leaf. The third man embraced its leg and said an elephant was like a pillar.

Like the blind men, Christians, scientists and society also differ about the cause of emotional problems because they consider only one or two factors to the exclusion of others. They fail to see that all the following can play a role: lack of willpower, sinful choices, the devil or evil forces, understanding of the issue, emotional development and upbringing, environment and traumatic events, and biology.

Many Christians deny or minimize the role of biological and developmental factors in causing emotional problems. They point out that sin, choice and will are the culprits in all these difficulties. Some blame the devil or demons as the cause of most problems. This extreme makes me just as uncomfortable as its opposite: that the devil has no influence in the world. Satan is certainly alive and well. But I usually "see" him working through the other avenues I have been describing, such as upbringing or environment. The apostle Paul stresses the need to maintain appropriate relationships so that we "do not give the devil an opportunity" (Eph 4:27).

Parents, especially mothers, have been blamed for many of the problems experienced by their children. A 1988 survey showed that 65 percent of the general population believe that mental illness is the result of bad parenting.[1] Parents certainly play a role, but it has probably been overemphasized. One woman in our church went through years of agony when she was accused of being a schizophrenogenic mother— that is, that her parenting was entirely responsible for producing her child's schizophrenia. Too many conscientious Christian parents today are blaming themselves for the actions of their wayward kids. One psychologist puts it aptly: "Parents probably deserve less credit for when things go well, and much less blame for problems."[2]

But Christians aren't the only ones with myopia. Many secular researchers talk only about nature or nurture as the cause, completely omitting the role of personal choice. William Glasser, quoted earlier, eventually went to the opposite extreme. In one of his later books, *Take Effective Control of Your Life,* he places almost 100 percent of the blame on personal choice.[3] Many therapists commit another grave error when they don't appreciate the spiritual dimension of their patients or clients.

Furthermore, some therapists (both Christian and non-Christian) focus primarily on one cause and fail to appreciate other, often multiple, factors influencing a given disorder. To ignore a basic cause of an emotional problem leads to catastrophe for the sufferer. Human suffering cannot be reduced to a simplistic formula. For the church to be most helpful, it must realize the diversity of causes afflicting the hurting people in its midst. That is the only way fellow Christians can be both compassionate and helpful.

I am pleading for balance! In the last few years I've seen within the Christian community an alarming tendency toward several extremes on the issue of causes: blaming all emotional difficulties on the willful sin of the victim, on demons, on parents or, at the other extreme, on purely psychological or biological factors.

No doubt all our problems started with original sin. As a result, every aspect of our lives has been affected—even the genes we pass on to our children. In addition, Satan influences us wherever he can—particularly in our areas of weakness. Yet people are helped most when they see that *all three areas*—choice, nature and nurture—contribute most significantly to our emotional problems.

More and more experts in the medical sciences are beginning to recognize the combination of causes. For example, E. J. Khantzian of Harvard Medical School says that alcoholism has multiple determinants, not just one cause. He further states that "human suffering . . . cannot be reduced to simplistic either-or conclusions."[4] The two leading organizations dealing with alcoholism recently revised their definitions, stating that "alcoholism is a primary, chronic disease with genetic, psychosocial, and environmental factors influencing its development and manifestations."[5] However, field researchers stop short of determinism: "No one is predestined to become an alcoholic, but genetic factors increase or decrease the level of vulnerability to this problem."[6]

Not "Whether," but "How Much"

With most emotional disorders, the cause is becoming much clearer. We are no longer asking *whether* biology or environment play a role, but *how much* of a role these and other factors play in a given disorder. One writer on genetics says, "For any particular disorder we need to come up with the right formula—how much is caused by the environment and how much is caused by genetics?"[7] I would add, "How much is a matter of the individual's choice?"

For the sake of discussion (and I believe it's close to being accurate) I am going to say that, *on the average,* each of the three factors plays about an equal role. That is, each contributes one-third of the cause. Figure 1 illustrates such a division and represents an average.

Regarding anxiety disorders, for example, one Swedish expert, Mats Humble, believes that genetic factors account for an average of 40 percent of their cause. Yet he also says that traumatic environmental

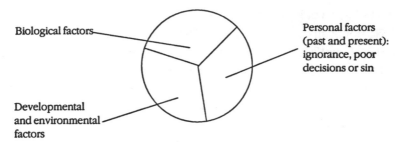

Figure 1. Average person with an emotional illness

factors trigger them, and thought processes and behavioral factors affect whether or not the symptoms continue and get better or worse.[8]

Remember Pat, who developed panic attacks after a flat tire? Her maternal grandmother and aunt had had panic attacks, and her mother had phobias. Her history suggests that a very strong genetic-biological vulnerability set the stage for her to develop panic attacks. In addition, her grandmother and mother often communicated their fears to Pat while she was growing up, thus adding the developmental influence. The threatening experience—being stuck on an unfamiliar street with all the graffiti and seeing the people of another ethnic group—provided the environmental factors that precipitated her first attack.

I saw Pat for the first time four months after her first attack. She was avoiding situations that might cause her to panic. Such avoidance behavior eliminates the immediate problem and decreases the panic attacks for the moment; but it also allows the fear to remain and in fact to grow. Pat did not know that her avoidance choices were becoming a factor in her problem. Even after we talked about how avoidance can make panic worse and I encouraged her to take steps to counteract it, she had a hard time following through on my assignments. Furthermore, she continued to feed her fears with the notion that she would "go loony tunes." Such "catastrophizing" leads to agoraphobia, the debilitating fear of having panic attacks. Since agoraphobia increasingly incapacitated her, I recommended some medications that often help. To date she has refused them—another choice.

In my estimation, about one-third of Pat's problem stems from her underlying biological vulnerability, another third from her upbringing and environmental factors, and the last third from choices for which she is responsible.

Let's look at another example—Skip, the minister's son who developed schizophrenia. With all the research on schizophrenia, I am convinced that predominantly biological factors caused his illness.[9] Yet his dad's pressures to stop his medications and the church's lack of support for Skip contribute a minimal part to his symptoms. Part of it also depends on Skip's doing what he can, including taking his medications. Figure 2 illustrates this situation.

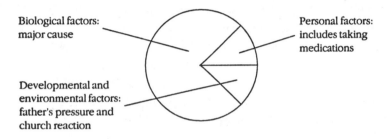

Biological factors:
major cause

Personal factors:
includes taking
medications

Developmental and
environmental factors:
father's pressure and
church reaction

Figure 2. Predominantly biological (physical) causes

In chapter six I told you about Dixie, the woman with insomnia who as a child had been molested by her father. Developmental factors appear to be the major cause of her current difficulties. I have not been able to identify any biological causes. Her personal responsibility mainly consists of her willingness to work on the problem now that it has been identified. Figure 3 illustrates her situation.

The most self-centered individual may be blatantly choosing his lifestyle, and so his own personal responsibility plays the principal role in his problem. However, even in these situations, the biological and environmental factors can still play a part. Consider Ron, who was running around with his bookkeeper. His father ran around on each of his three wives; several of his brothers had similar traits, as did his grandfather. Ron's mother was a controlling person with a strong family history of alcoholism.

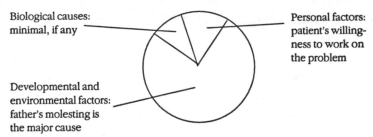

Biological causes:
minimal, if any

Personal factors:
patient's willing-
ness to work on
the problem

Developmental and
environmental factors:
father's molesting is
the major cause

Figure 3. Predominantly developmental environmental causes

It is impossible to know for sure how much of Ron's personality derived from some biological influence, but it certainly was influenced by developmental factors. A fair estimate might be 10 percent biological and 30 percent developmental influences. Hopefully, this view will give us some empathy for Ron. On the other hand, 60 percent of the cause of his problem lies in his own choices. He *can* choose to stop running around and choose to actively work on his marriage. God holds him responsible for his choices, even though other factors are involved. Figure 4 illustrates the factors for Ron.

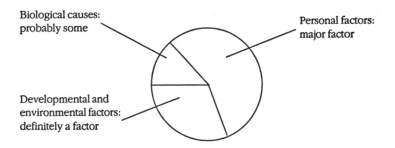

Biological causes:
probably some

Personal factors:
major factor

Developmental and
environmental factors:
definitely a factor

Figure 4. Predominantly individual's choice

I trust you can see from these examples that the cause of an illness can be complex. In fact, only God knows for sure the exact causes of a specific person's illness. Furthermore, though an illness may appear to be the same in two different people—that is, they both have the same symptoms—the causes may be different.

Why is it so important to be aware of the multiple factors that may lead to emotional illness? First, because *appreciating these facts will help us to be less judging of ourselves or others,* thus reducing the stigma associated with these diseases. Second, because *a better understanding of the cause of an illness can lead to hope in correcting it.* As in all of medicine, knowing the cause of the disorder is the first step in remedying it.

Let me illustrate this second point. Diabetes generally has a genetic basis, though factors such as a poor diet and being overweight can make it worse. Since my dad has diabetes, I may have a genetic tendency to get the disease. I also like sweets, and if I were ever to develop diabetes, I could feel some guilt over whether I had caused it. But since I know the facts about its genetic basis, I will not blame myself for causing it. Instead, I will devote my energies to doing all I can to minimize its effects.

Knowing the true causes helps alleviate a lot of personal guilt so people can instead devote all their energy to dealing with the illness itself. Diabetics can keep their weight under control and avoid extreme temperatures that could damage their fingers and toes. They can maintain a regular schedule and diet and avoid undue stress. All of this, as well as taking insulin if necessary, is under their control and will keep them alive.

* * *

My prayer is that we in Christendom will develop a greater understanding and a more helpful approach to people with emotional difficulties—one that will neither let people evade choices they need to make nor add guilt to the burden they are already carrying. Instead, it will help them sort out the various causes, seek appropriate help and feel the support of their church community throughout their journey toward health and wholeness.

PART III

How Shall the Wounded Be Mended?

J ESUS ASKED LAZARUS'S FRIENDS TO UNBIND HIM AFTER HE CAME OUT OF THE tomb. So too, he asks those of us around the emotionally ill to unbind them with love, acceptance and nurture.

The church has the power to increase its members' emotional difficulties or alleviate them—to be part of the problem or part of the solution. If the church will be the loving community described in Scripture, it can play a tremendous therapeutic role in the lives of people who, though spiritually resurrected, are still bound by physical weakness and emotional illness. Further, individual Christians who are strong can learn to help the weak—if they are willing to become aware of their own weaknesses.

— 9 —

The Church: Business, School or Hospital?

TOO MANY CHURCHES TODAY ARE FILLED WITH EXECUTIVES WHO GET together to talk about the bottom line. Most churches have their measures of "success": a certain number of converts, a specified increase in "giving units," a "star" pastor or youth leader, an array of flashy programs, or the numerical growth of the congregation. When we focus on these external things, however, all too often we neglect and inadvertently hurt the wounded among us. We need to be more like a hospital and a school: nurturing the injured and equipping the saints.

I had set aside the day to work on this chapter. But when a patient called and told me he'd had a terrible week, I left the house to go meet him at my office. Pete is in his midtwenties, is married and has several children. Most people would think he has no difficulties, but he struggles with symptoms of anxiety and an obsessive-compulsive disorder. In addition, severe headaches and nausea often torment him.

Last week Pete decided to share his struggles with Bill, one of his bosses at work who is a Christian. Pete thought Bill would understand;

instead he got a sermon. "God wants you well," Bill proclaimed, "and the choice is *totally* yours, Pete, whether you want to remain in distress or be free from it." This "exhortation" sent Pete into a nosedive. His symptoms worsened, he was unable to go to work, and he became fearful of seeing his "Christian brother."

Bill responded to Pete this way because he comes from a church that is enamored with numbers. Furthermore, this church's "emotional prosperity gospel" has little tolerance for those who hurt. Its view of the cause of all emotional problems boils down to "it's all your fault."

Drawing from the material in this book, I was able to show Pete that a large portion of his illness is biological and that he should not accept the false guilt that Bill was dumping on him. This enabled Pete to return to work, to handle his emotional symptoms more constructively and to deal with Bill's false conclusions.

Rocks and Seeds

In the above situation, Pete wasn't the only one in need. Bill also needed help in gaining a balanced view of emotional illness. What can we do to help *both* the Petes and the Bills in our congregations? To start with, we must remember the difference between a rock and a seed. In the parable of the sower (Mt 13; Mk 4; Lk 8), the seed, which represents the Word, is sown on four types of ground. The crucial variable isn't the seed, but the preparation of the soil. Though the seed is totally sufficient to produce a healthy plant, when it is sown on rocky soil, the seedling cannot continue to grow after it springs up.

In this case the only fault is that the rocks hadn't been cleared away first. I believe these rocks can represent old childhood injuries and wounds. Those with such old hurts may receive the Word with joy but quickly "fall away" because "they have no firm root in themselves"—that is, they didn't receive the necessary nurturing in their early lives. And just as the farmer is needed to clear away the rocks in the parable, the church needs to help its hurting members clear away the "rocks" in their lives so their emotional and spiritual health can be nourished. The Word and Christ are certainly sufficient, but the church must acknowledge and deal with the reality of "rocks" if these people in our congregations are to grow in the Lord.

To Unbind and to Mend

As I compare the resurrections of Christ and Lazarus, I find a significant difference that speaks to our healing processes today. Jesus slipped out of his tightly bound graveclothes without the help or witness of anyone; Lazarus needed assistance. Jesus did the impossible for Lazarus, but he asked others to do the possible—to "unbind" Lazarus from his wrappings. In the same manner, God does the supernatural when he gives us spiritual life. But often he leaves it to the church and sometimes to healing professionals to untangle us from the weaknesses, infirmities and harmful habits that bind us. Rather than increase our bondage with false guilt and rejection, the church needs to be a part of the unbinding process.

In addition to unbinding those who hurt, the church needs to mend their lives. In other words, the church should be a hospital for those who are suffering. Ephesians 4:11-14 says:

And he gave some, apostles; and some, prophets; and some, evangelists, and some, pastors and teachers; For the perfecting of the saints, for the work of the ministry, for the edifying of the body of Christ: Till we all come in the unity of the faith, and of the knowledge of the Son of God, unto a perfect man, unto the measure of the stature of the fulness of Christ: That we henceforth be no more children. (KJV)

For years I assumed that the church and Christian leaders were supposed to encourage "perfection" in all Christians. More recently I have learned the original meaning of the Greek word *katartismos*. The King James translates this word in Ephesians 4:12 as the *perfecting* of the saints; in the New American Standard and other versions it is rendered *equipping*. In other portions of the Scriptures it is translated as *completing* and, in Galatians 6:1, as *restoring*.

The Greek root from which *katartismos* is derived means "to mend." In Matthew 4:21, where James and John are "mending" their nets, we find this same root word. In that day it was also used in medicine and meant "to set a broken bone."

Today *perfecting* has a different connotation. It conjures up the idea of something or someone who has almost arrived, or is putting on the finishing touches. *Equipping* and *completing* make me think of adding some quality that is lacking. *Mending* brings to mind something that is broken, defective, unable to function correctly, in need of repair. As we examine Jesus' life, isn't *mending* what we find him doing most? He consistently cared for the broken and hurting. When Mary cried at the death of her brother, Jesus wept with her, even though he had ample reason to tell her to stop, since he knew he would raise Lazarus from the dead. He showed compassion to troubled people—the woman caught in adultery, people stricken with leprosy, the poor and hungry and crippled, and many others.

Not Perfect Yet
Some might counter that we already extend that kind of compassion to the needy in our congregations. Certainly some individuals and churches practice this grace of restoring the brokenhearted. But in general, we are often more accepting of non-Christians in our midst (as long as they don't dress differently or do something offensive). We accept their past life of sin and rejoice when they accept Christ—and then we probably give them, on the average, one to six months to get their lives in order. After that we begin to convey a subtle (and sometimes not-so-subtle) form of disapproval if they fail to measure up to our standards of Christian behavior and appearance.

Before long they realize that to be accepted in the congregation, they must perform. Any resentments, struggles, spiritual questions or emotional problems "should" be things of the past. And if they need to see a therapist or take any medication—that is anathema. Their ticket to full acceptance in the church is "I'm Joe, I was a sinner but now I'm saved!"—the implication being "I've got it all together." What a contrast with the attitude of those in Alcoholics Anonymous! Their ticket for acceptance is "I'm Joe, a *recovering* alcoholic"—in other words, "I *don't* have it all together."

Henry Cloud, in *When Your World Makes No Sense,* comments on this phenomenon:

It is interesting to compare a legalistic church with a good AA group. In the church, it is culturally unacceptable to have problems; that is called being sinful. In the AA group, it is culturally unacceptable to be perfect; that is called denial. In one setting people look better but get worse, and in the other, they look worse but get better.[1]

With this kind of denial a Christian fellowship can never reach a deeper level of honesty and openness. Dietrich Bonhoeffer says:

The final break-through [to honesty] does not occur, because . . . the pious fellowship permits no one to be a sinner. So everybody must conceal his sin from himself and from the fellowship. We dare not be sinners. Many Christians are unthinkably horrified when a real sinner is suddenly discovered among the righteous. So we remain alone with our sin, living in lies and hypocrisy. The fact is that we *are* sinners![2]

We all still battle with our sinful nature. Paul describes his battle in Romans 7:15: "For that which I am doing, I do not understand; for I am not practicing what I would like to do, but I am doing the very thing I hate." Then he goes on to acknowledge that "the Spirit also helps our *weakness"* (Rom 8:26). The King James Version renders the word *weakness* as *infirmities.* In fact, one of the refreshing things about God's Word is its candid honesty about the ongoing weaknesses in the lives of those who follow God.

We all fall short all the time if we are honest with ourselves. Who is able for a day to have "perfect faith" or to be "perfect," "holy" or "totally loving" as the Scriptures command? Further, the person with an emotional illness doesn't necessarily sin more than one without emotional illness.

We all constantly need the redemptive forgiveness of Jesus Christ. The gap between the ideal and our actual performance can only be filled by God's grace. We simply cannot earn any spiritual "points." As the classic hymn puts it, "Nothing in my hand I bring / Simply to Thy cross I cling." Bonhoeffer goes on to assure his readers that "[God] wants you as you are. . . . The mask you wear before men will do you no good before Him."[3] You can dare to admit you're a sinner because God loves you just as you are.

The church will not be the nurturing hospital it needs to be for hurting people until it more fully appreciates that we are all redeemed sinners who still struggle. Only as the entire church recognizes its continual need for God's mercy and grace will it be a caring and supportive place for those who suffer emotionally.

When it is a gracious place, the church can help the hurting immensely by providing love, acceptance and nurturing. These graces can only be conveyed, however, in an environment where the suffering person is free to be known—where everyone knows and accepts that we all struggle.

Critics Agree on the Need

Even those most critical of the field of Christian psychology appreciate the tremendous need in the church to help the hurting. Dave Hunt writes:

We would not minimize the sad fact that many of the sheep in Christ's flock are weak and bruised and in need of help that too often they are not receiving. . . . One of the most desperate needs within the church is for personal and family and marriage counseling. . . . Only when the church considers *counseling* of individuals to be as important as *preaching* to and *teaching* congregations will biblical counseling take its rightful place in the church. Until then the best sermons will still leave many practical needs unmet. . . .

The healing of broken lives, moreover, cannot be accomplished by an hour of counseling once or even several times a week. It can take place only in the context of the caring and loving family of God, the body of Christ concerned for the welfare of each member.[4]

Along similar lines, John MacArthur says:

I would not for a moment dispute the important role of those who are spiritually gifted to offer encouragement, discernment, comfort, advice, compassion, and help to others. In fact, one of the very problems that has led to the current plague of bad counsel is that churches have not done as well as they could in enabling people with those kinds of spiritual gifts to minister excellently. The complexities of this modern age make it more difficult than ever to take the time necessary to listen well, serve others through compassionate personal involvement, and otherwise provide the close fellowship necessary for the church body to enjoy health and vitality.[5]

I couldn't agree more heartily with these statements. Not only have we injured the wounded, but so often we have not helped them in their suffering. To truly recognize this sad situation is to take a major step toward improving it.

Now let's turn our attention to some specific ways the church can minister to the wounded among us.

Safe Places for Parishioners

We all know the Scriptures teach that God loves and cares for us. But our early development can greatly affect the way we *perceive* him. Those who lacked a warm, loving home environment, whose nurturing failed to communicate that they were loved and innately valuable, find it almost impossible to recognize and receive God's love and care on their own. Usually they first need to experience love and caring through another human being. So our emotional growth depends on a warm, nurturing relationship, which in turn affects our spiritual growth.

Jean comes to mind. She is twenty-nine and a deeply committed Christian with a fantastic knowledge of God's Word. Nevertheless, she was in emotional and spiritual turmoil. Her upbringing was nonnurturing, and she usually felt "no good and empty inside." Early in her treatment I expressed that God loved and cared for her—even if she didn't feel it from him and never felt it from her parents. She angrily retorted, "That's not good enough—I need a God with skin on."

I understood what she meant. So for months I tried to be God's representative "with skin on." She repeatedly tested me by expressing her anger at God and her father in my presence. She would pound on the arms of the chair with her fists and yell so loudly that it hurt my ears. And though my office walls are somewhat soundproof, my colleague and his patient in the next room could hear her shouting. I wondered what they might think I was doing to her. I thought many times about asking her to tone down her voice, but I decided not to.

Her raging continued on and off over several months of therapy. I communicated my acceptance of her as a person and tried in our sessions to be the nurturing, stable human being that she had never had. She needed someone "with skin on" who would accept and nurture her until she was able to take the next step of growth in her life.

A few months later she had a gradual but phenomenal breakthrough in which she forgave and felt reconciled with both her father and God.

I believe this process of experiencing total acceptance is exactly the message of Ephesians 3:17-19:

> And I pray that you, *firmly fixed in love yourselves,* may be able to grasp (with all Christians) how wide and deep and long and high is the love of Christ—and to know that love for yourselves. May you be filled through all your being with God Himself! (Phillips; italics mine)

In other words, we grow best when we have been rooted in an atmosphere of genuine human love; this seems to be a prerequisite for comprehending the greatness of God's love.

But those who did not experience unconditional love as a child often need a corrective experience, a nurturing environment in which they feel fully accepted—often for the first time in their life. They also need to uncover both the facts and the feelings of past hurts; and they need a safe place to express and sort them out and still be accepted by other human beings.

But how can those who are hurting feel fully accepted? To begin the process, the church must acknowledge that emotional illness is present among us, and that it is not all due to the sufferers' personal sin. When that fact is accepted, the hurting people can begin to share their feelings of pain, emptiness, anger—all the negative feelings that seemed so "bad." Then, as things that have been perceived as "bad" are exposed, the church community still needs to tangibly express that it fully accepts the sufferers. Finally, when the sufferers experience the kind of acceptance that has been tested and proven reliable—instead of the rejection they had always known—they will begin to believe in a God "with skin on."

In James 5:16 we read about this accepting aspect of Christian community from another perspective. Here the author gives instruction on how to minister to those who are suffering and sick. We are to confess our faults to one another (some translations say "trespasses" or "sins") and to pray for one another in order that we may be healed.

Open confession and compassionate prayer are what the church should be about—open about our faults, sins and areas of weakness. What better place is there to be restored than in a loving, caring group of Christians who admit their weaknesses and support and encourage each other? The psalmist writes, "Thou hast given me *room* when I was in distress" (Ps 4:1 RSV).

Supportive Friendships

Scores of studies have assessed both the needs of the emotionally distressed person and the benefits of supportive relationships. They found that the most important positive factor in the emotional improvement of wounded people is the *quality* of a supportive relationship.[6] But what are the essential ingredients in such a relationship?

First, struggling persons need a trustworthy, confidential relationship. They need at least one person with whom they can feel close in order to discuss personal matters. The person might be a spouse, parent or friend.

Second, they need one or more friends with whom they can freely express their feelings without any sense of criticism or judgment. The hurting person needs to be accepted with empathy. The confidant must be a good listener, someone who will truly hear the other person. The listener needs to empathize—that is, "feel with" the hurting individual.

Third, they need someone who can "feel with" them without getting emotionally entangled. The illness or emotional problems should never alter the relationship. For instance, if hospitalization became necessary, the friend would be able to remain a consistent friend during and after the hospital stay.

Fourth, hurting people need a strong, positive, nonpatronizing role model. "Strong" doesn't mean free of problems, but rather reliable and modeling a hopeful, realistic working-through of problems. There also needs to be a sense of partnership.

Fifth, wounded people sometimes need practical, tangible assistance such as baby-sitting, a ride to the doctor's office, a bag of groceries or possibly even loans or gifts of money at times.

Sixth, they need encouragement. It should never be given in such a way, however, that it minimizes their feelings or causes them to feel they haven't been heard. For example, to say, "Don't worry, everything will be O.K." glosses over the person's feelings and doesn't really help. To say, "I know this is a hard time for you and I'll stand by you" is much more helpful.

Seventh, at times wounded people need information and feedback. Many lack basic knowledge about life in general, as well as spiritual knowledge. There is a place for concrete suggestions, feedback and guidance. Such guidance may include recommending ways to find better jobs or housing, explaining legal or insurance forms, or helping to evaluate the wisdom of a given decision. However, one must be careful to keep this aspect of the relationship in perspective: all too often Christians pour on the advice and neglect the other aspects of a supportive relationship.[7]

Specialized Supportive Relationships

Despite the quality of their friendships in the church, some people still need the support of others who have experienced the same kinds of difficulties they are going through. The most tangible way a church can express its acceptance and help for the hurting is by offering care groups and specialized support groups.

One such group is Overcomers, begun in 1985 by Bob and Pauline Bartosch. Though he had been a leader in his church, Bob was an alcoholic, and he knew he needed help. (He now refers to himself as a recovering alcoholic.) So he and Pauline started a Christian Twelve-Step program similar to Alcoholics Anonymous, but with a Christ-centered emphasis. In its first seven years Overcomers mushroomed into one thousand groups in forty-nine U.S. states and ten other countries. Many of the groups meet in churches. Its growth shows the tremendous need for hurting people to gather regularly and support each other.

There are many other support groups that a church could sponsor. In our church we have a group for those from dysfunctional families, an anxiety support group, a "Tough Love" group for parents with wayward children and a group for those with non-Christian spouses, as well as the more typical groups for widows, seniors and so on.

Many fellowships now train lay Christian counselors, who can be a tremendous asset to the body of Christ. In addition, pastors and lay leaders need to educate themselves on the support groups available in their areas. They should also feel free to refer parishioners to a support group or lay counselors in another church if that would help them.

Whether or not a person attends one of these groups, every parishioner needs some safe place to share their struggles, regardless of the specific need. An atmosphere of acceptance should eventually permeate every area of the church. As this happens we will become better able to pray for and support one another.

The Church Can't Meet Every Need

When the church fosters openness in an atmosphere of love, many more of its members' needs are addressed. As it is, many go to a therapist to find someone who will accept them unconditionally. Until the church becomes that safe haven, we will continue to rely on the many godly professionals I believe God has given us to help the emotionally distressed. In addition, certain people struggling with more tenacious difficulties will always need professional help.

Much of the Christian community is beginning to realize that some people in every church, regardless of its size or maturity, need this extra help. I know it sounds unscriptural to say that some individuals need more than the church can offer. However, if your car needs the transmission replaced, you don't expect the church to do it. Or if you break your leg, you consult with a physician, not with your pastor. But when it comes to emotional needs, we think the church should be able to meet them all. It can't, and it isn't supposed to.

The church is, or at least should be, expert in spiritual counseling. Appropriate spiritual counseling will resolve issues such as salvation, forgiveness, personal morality, God's will, the scriptural perspective on divorce and more. It can also help some emotional difficulties. But many emotional or mental illnesses (especially those with a clinical diagnosis and a primarily physical basis) require more than a church support network can offer.

Confusion between the spiritual and the emotional spheres invariably stirs up great turmoil in a struggling person, which in turn can create false guilt, depression and more distress. It may also lead to inappropriate treatment, which often leads to disappointment with God, if not a flat-out rejection of both God and the church.

Church leaders can alleviate some of the confusion by getting to know Christian therapists in their communities to whom they can refer people with a persistent emotional problem. Have lunch with the counselors and find out what they believe and what kind of therapy they practice, so that when a need arises in your congregation you will already know to whom you can refer the person. Forty percent of all individuals who need emotional help seek it first from the church; some of these need to be referred to a mental health professional. (For a number of reasons it is best to supply several different names when a referral is needed—which makes it especially important to get to know a range of therapists.)

It is crucial that we work together to use all our resources—as pastors, church leaders, support groups and professional counselors—to assist emotionally hurting people. If professionals and church leaders can see each other's valuable role, we will make progress in helping the wounded. If we take potshots at each other, the wounded will be further injured in the crossfire. We must work together.

Stop the Polarization

Many popular writers and communicators make their point by overstatement. They set forth a stronger position than they really believe or practice in order to sell their books or (they hope) to bring the masses into better balance. Some just like a good fight.

As I read *Beyond Seduction* and *Our Sufficiency in Christ,* I believe both authors make some excellent points. But their opposition to Christian psychology is at best an overstatement and at worst causing division in the body of Christ. Rather than restore balance to most of evangelical Christianity, books such as these have polarized the body of Christ. We end up fighting against each other instead of our common enemy.

A recent issue of *Moody Monthly* dealt with the debate over Christian counseling. Several writers took a strong stand against it. But Joseph M. Stowell, president of Moody Bible Institute, wrote a balanced article. It said in part:

> There is often a need for well-trained counselors to lead the broken to healing.
>
> Does that mean the Scripture and the Spirit are not sufficient? No. . . . While much that is taught and practiced in secular counseling is unbiblical, it is also true that there are many helpful insights to be gleaned from this field. . . .
>
> We live in a season when life is increasingly complex and the fragility of precious souls is demonstrated by growing brokenness and complicated conflicts. We dare not waste their sorrows on the battlefield of careless counsel that violates biblical parameters or with simplistic, unqualified solutions that plunge them ultimately into deeper despair.[8]

Hurrah for Joseph Stowell. I am sure that Mary, Pete and Jean (mentioned earlier in this chapter) would say "amen." The crying need is for a community in the body of Christ where there is love, acceptance, encouragement, forgiveness and compassion, where the person of Christ is lifted high and God's Word is never compromised—but also where there is openness to use all available methods that are not contrary to his Word. Only then will we be able to work together, to avoid schism and criticism, and to foster spiritual, emotional and physical growth.

— 10 —

How the Strong Can Help— Not Shoot—the Wounded

R EMEMBER JERRI? IN CHAPTER FOUR I DESCRIBED HOW SHE BENEFITED FROM a new medication for obsessive-compulsive disorder. However, she couldn't bring herself to share the news with her minister for fear of his disapproval. After reading a manuscript of this book, Jerri told me, "If only my pastor could understand this and not give pat answers—his ministry could be greatly increased." I suspect Jerri's assessment would apply to many "strong" Christian leaders around the country.

Most of my patients do not tell their pastor or key leaders in the church, or for that matter even their close friends, that they are getting psychological help. Why? And how can the church move toward helping rather than hindering these wounded saints?

First and foremost, the tremendous prejudice and inaccurate informa- tion I have covered in the previous nine chapters must be appreciated by the "strong" in our congregations.

CEO or Shepherd?

In recent years many of our senior pastors have become less like shepherds and more like chief executive officers. This trend has frightening consequences for the already hurting. As in large corporations, the "bottom line"—growth, success, dollars—becomes the all-important objective, and young, awkward lambs will get in the way. I hope we will never deserve the criticism God gave to the shepherds of Israel:

> Those who are sickly you have not strengthened, the diseased you have not healed, the broken you have not bound up, the scattered you have not brought back, nor have you sought for the lost; but with force and with severity you have dominated them. And they were scattered for lack of a shepherd, and they became food for every beast of the field and were scattered. (Ezek 34:4-5)

My wife is a dedicated Christian; after completing nurses' training, she became area leader for a Christian organization, discipling other women. But being sensitive and at times struggling, in private she went to a Christian leader—a person whose name most American evangelicals would readily recognize—and shared her questions. He responded, "It's conceivable that you have never been born again."

The wound this man inflicted on my wife scarred her for decades. To this day I am sure that he remains unaware of the damage he did.

There are other comments that wound:

☐ "If you yield your life to Jesus, you will never need psychological help."

☐ "It's a sin to be anxious."

☐ "The need for medications is from the devil."

Even everyday, seemingly insignificant challenges can wound the sensitive person: pleas for people to volunteer as Christian workers, or challenges to go witnessing door to door, may hurt some. There is no end to the ways one can injure a lamb. Shepherds must always consider the effects of their words and actions on the weakest parishioner—else they will wound.

A doctor would never go into the waiting room and give everyone the same prescription; a teacher in a one-room schoolhouse would not give every child, from first to eighth grade, the same assignments. Each patient needs an individualized prescription; each child needs work appropriate to his or her grade level. Preaching and recruiting should follow the same principle.

Jesus, the Good Shepherd, had tremendous empathy for all and tailored his responses to the needs of each person. Although he instructed the rich young ruler to sell everything and follow him, he told the Gadarene demoniac *not* to follow him, but to go home. When Zacchaeus volunteered to give to the poor and repay everything he had stolen, Jesus laid no demands upon him. And when Lazarus died, Jesus reasoned with Martha but wept with Mary.

The strong—whether senior pastor, youth pastor, elder, Bible study leader or average church member—must remember Christ's warning about causing "one of these little ones to stumble." Many among us are "little ones" emotionally; we must not look down on them or in some way derail their healing process (Mt 18:5-6, 10-14; Mk 9:36-42; Lk 17:1-2).

The Need for Transparency

The strongest among us must communicate their weaknesses; else they will continue to perpetuate the erroneous conclusion that "they've got it all together." We all struggle with at least some areas of weakness, as Paul Tournier emphasizes in *The Strong and the Weak:* "The truth is that human beings are much more alike than they think. What is different is the external mask, sparkling or disagreeable, their outward reaction, strong or weak. Their appearances, however, hide an identical inner personality. . . . All men, in fact, are weak. All are weak because all are afraid."[1]

Even the "strong" need to be transparent about some less-than-perfect aspects of their lives. Transparency is necessary, not only to maintain their own emotional and spiritual health but also to foster an environment where the "weaker brother" will feel safe. The creation of such an environment must start in the pulpit and permeate the ranks of everyone in the church. Allowing others to see our fears and weaknesses scares us—but it opens a channel for authentic community and genuine growth. The Scriptures are full of such examples of transparency. Moses was able to express openly his strong feelings of inadequacy; David was very honest about his personal struggles. When James tells us to confess our faults to one another and to pray for one another, he didn't say "*if* you have faults." God knows we all have faults—the question is whether we are aware of them and willing to share them.

The Need for Patience

In chapter three I discussed 1 Thessalonians 5:14, which says to the strong, "And we urge you, brethren, admonish the unruly, encourage the fainthearted, help the weak, be patient with all men." This passage acknowledges the presence of individuals with all kinds of weaknesses. We are to be supportive and tender with them. Note that the verse gives no indication that these deficiencies will be resolved in a week, a month or a year. In many instances both the strong and the weak need to accept the reality of lifelong deficiencies, or else we fail to "be patient with all men." Charles Wanamaker concludes that the reason we must "be patient toward everyone" is that "such people often become irritating and burdensome to those who seek to care for them."[2] Biblical scholar Ernest Best writes: "It is all too easy to lose patience . . . [with] the *worried* and the *weak* even when admonishing or assisting them; and there are many others who will try [our] patience. . . . Hence the necessity for a call for restraint from anger towards all who upset the sweet running of the [Christian] community."[3]

Unload Before You Shoot

Recently at a wedding reception I spoke with a woman whom I deeply respect as an emotionally and spiritually healthy person. She asked me about my activities, and I told her about this book I was writing on how Christians tend to shoot their wounded. She replied: "I can understand why some would shoot the wounded—in fact, sometimes I feel like doing just that. I have a number of friends who are wounded, and it seems that their problems go on and on and on—and it wears me out."

Though her comment may seem unkind, I understood where she was coming from. As a trained professional I have learned that I can handle only a limited amount of emotional "weight." Some of my colleagues can handle more than I can—but I must carefully limit my practice. I have discovered that I can handle no more than twenty-five to thirty patient contact hours per week; otherwise I start to burn out. And among these clients I can handle only about three individuals who present a diagnostic challenge—those who are seriously suicidal or who in some other way demand a lot from me. Thus I have to turn away many more patients than I can accept—and that is hard. They are often very wounded individuals, and often they plead to be accepted, saying that I am the only human who can help them. Whether their claim is true I do not know. But I do know that I must maintain sufficient emotional strength to help those I've already accepted into my practice, reserve time for my family, set aside at least a little time for myself and other Christian commitments and, most important, keep time for my personal relationship with God. I am sure I am misunderstood at times when I limit my patient load, but I know it is absolutely necessary.

No matter how strong, capable or well-trained you might be, you are still human and have limitations. Whether you are strong or weak (the weak frequently get into this bind also), you must know your capacity to help the hurting and strive to limit your involvement long before you exceed your limit.

Moses was advised that the burden of God's children was too much for him and that he needed to delegate the responsibility to others lest he burn out (Ex 18:13-24). Christ told his disciples to "come away by yourselves to a lonely place and rest a while" (Mk 6:31). They rested despite the fact that the multitudes were clamoring for their help.

If you exceed your limitations, I can almost guarantee that you will end up hurting yourself, your loved ones and the very ones you are trying to help. A minister I am seeing now "can't say no" to someone in need; not only is he burned out and depressed as a result, but periodically he also deeply injures one of the people he is trying to help.

Emotionally hurting people can be very needy and draining. So you may have to limit the number of individuals you become more deeply involved with, or limit the amount of energy or time you spend with them. In fact, if you don't do this, at some point you can become codependent with them and their problems. In such a situation, even though it appears that you are loving or helping, you may actually make their problems worse. If you don't "unload the gun," your finger is likely to slip and you'll end up shooting yourself or the wounded you are trying to help.

If you are already approaching the limit of your own capacity, the preferable way to "unload" is to avoid getting involved with additional people in need. Such situations must be handled in a gentle, gracious manner. It is also important to set limits on your involvement with even one extremely needy person. With God's help, decide to what extent you are able to help. Maybe you can meet with him or her weekly for several hours to share concerns and pray—but you know you cannot spend six hours a week. If done lovingly but firmly, setting guidelines can potentially be more helpful to the person—as well as to yourself— than meeting the person's every request.

A word to pastors: To help the more deeply wounded individuals in your congregation takes a tremendous amount of time and emotional energy. I believe your first priority is to give yourself to the Word, to prayer and to the spiritual growth of your flock (Acts 6:2-4). If you will truly accept the hurting in your midst and avoid pat answers for difficult problems, you will help immeasurably. But limit your actual time helping those with deeper emotional difficulties, refer when necessary, and encourage others in your congregation to be available to help those with emotional needs.

*   *   *

The strong play a pivotal role in providing an atmosphere of acceptance, love, understanding and help for the weaker brother and sister. Only with the ambiance of the tender touch of the shepherd will the scared and injured lambs feel safe enough to come out of their places of hiding and get the help they so desperately need. As the Scriptures so aptly state: "Now we who are strong ought to bear the weaknesses of those without strength and not just please ourselves" (Rom 15:1).

— 11 —

What the Wounded Can Do While the Bullets Are Flying

T HE STATEMENT "ONLY CHRISTIANS SHOOT THEIR WOUNDED" CHALLENGED me to write this book. It was made by a colleague who had seen some missionaries go to great lengths to deny that they had any emotional problems. I continually marvel at how hard it is for us to admit our weaknesses, especially since it is so crucial for us to be honest about our condition before God. Just as the first step to spiritual healing involves recognizing we are sinners, the first step to emotional healing involves recognizing we have emotional weaknesses.

Generally speaking, we first need to be honest with ourselves about the secrets that often seem so horrible. These secrets are often true at some level, but when we keep them hidden, they usually take on a life of their own and get exaggerated in our minds. Only when admitting their presence can we begin to assess their true size and shape. Honesty with ourselves is necessary in order to take the next step of being honest before God. Then we can open ourselves to the Holy Spirit's guidance regarding the existence and causes of our problems.

David exemplified this kind of open attitude toward his weaknesses in Psalm 139:23-24: "Search me, O God, and know my heart; Try me and know my anxious thoughts; And see if there be any hurtful way in me, And lead me in the everlasting way." After being honest with ourselves and with God, objective assessment and healing often requires us to be honest with at least one other human being.

Prayer, Obedience and Personal Responsibility

If your problem is strictly a spiritual one, its answer lies in God's Word. Sin needs to be confessed and forsaken (1 Jn 1:9). Learning to apply Scripture to your daily life can solve many of life's problems. The fact that I am not spending pages and pages on this point in no way means that I minimize it. It is a "given" and extremely important.

Suffering with an emotional illness doesn't alter your need to be obedient to God's expressed will. This obedience includes prayerfully seeking his guidance in how to deal with the problem. As discussed in earlier chapters, personal sin may not be at the root of your particular problem, but there still may be some areas in which you have a responsibility to help remedy the situation.

A number of friends, colleagues, ministers and patients who were kind enough to read this manuscript gave me interesting and helpful feedback. However, at times they differed strongly on what they wished I would emphasize. Their differences were particularly evident in the arena of personal responsibility. The stronger Christian leaders wanted me to make it exceedingly clear that even though we may have weaknesses or infirmities, they are never an excuse to sin. To this I say a hearty "amen." They also stressed that I needed to clearly delineate personal responsibility: God does not hold us responsible for what we can't help, but only for what we can do something about. Again I say "amen."

The real dilemma is that the healthy person who is functioning well can clearly see what he or she is responsible for, without being inundated with false guilt. But the emotionally distressed person can easily be overwhelmed by false guilt originating from either within or without. The account of Pete and his Christian friend in chapter nine illustrates the way false guilt can muddle one's thinking.

The challenge for all of us is to be understanding and gentle with the *broken* believer—even if sin and personal responsibility are involved—but not to be "soft" on the sin itself. This tightrope is difficult to walk. Those continuing in sin are responsible for the choices they make. The Christian community should show them compassion and kindness that will facilitate their obedience to God's truth. Then they will be better able to sense God's acceptance and understanding of their predicament, as well as his desire to help them do all they are able to do.

Our Faith Enables

As I have already elaborated, our faith in the sufficiency of Christ does not guarantee physical or emotional health. Nevertheless, applying God's laws can actually enhance our physical health; some new studies indicate it can help us emotionally. In fact, individuals with a deep spiritual commitment do have better mental health, are more likely to have a sense of well-being, are less depressed and are less likely to take their own lives. When their religious faith is central, people have been shown to handle other physical illnesses in a more constructive manner.[1]

Seek a Caring Body of Believers

What's the difference between people and lobsters? Human beings are soft and warm on the outside with a hard skeleton on the inside; lobsters are soft and vulnerable inside but wear a hard shell on the outside. The church needs to be more like people: the skeleton of solid beliefs on the inside, but warm and huggable on the outside. Who needs a church like a lobster—hard and sharp—even if it is doctrinally "right"? The crustacean may be safe inside its armor, but no one wants to hug a lobster![2]

A nurturing, gracious, transparent Christian church is crucial for your spiritual and emotional growth. I have seen many dedicated Christians stymied in their spiritual and emotional growth because they don't receive the nurture of a gracious environment. Their fellowship may be doctrinally sound, but the people are harsh, legalistic and judgmental.

It seems as though I always have one or two patients who are sincere

Christians but come from very rigid churches where they do not experience grace. I generally attempt to help them grow within their fellowship. But try as they will, it seems that the fellowship stifles their lives. Sometimes the only way they can grow in their appreciation of God's grace is to find a body of believers who practice grace more. In such a fellowship it will be safer to be open and transparent. Hopefully the new fellowship will include some Christians who are stronger—who have worked through enough of their own struggles to be available emotionally for the weak.

Another important step for you who are weak is to find one friend who will accept you and not judge you as being an "unvictorious Christian." Here you will have to take the difficult risk of being vulnerable; you will have to share something of yourself that you are afraid to talk about. Don't take giant leaps at first; take small steps to "test the waters" and see how the person handles what you reveal about yourself. Hopefully, he or she will prove to be a caring, understanding and confidential friend. Over time, as your relationship grows, you can begin to share more deeply and perhaps find the nurturing relationship you need. If the first such relationship doesn't work out, don't give up; try another. Eventually, you will be able to find several with whom you can be yourself and still be fully accepted.

Closely related to this process is the need to find a group of people with whom you are accepted. This might be any one of the groups within your church such as a care group or a Sunday-school class. Also, look for an appropriate support group either in your church or in your community. If nothing seems to click, you might do what one of my patients did: she got two friends and they formed their own prayer and sharing group. The important thing is that you start to let others know who you really are and that they accept you and foster your genuine growth. Then you will discover that you can gradually venture out to become a more authentic person.

Be Willing to Seek Professional Help
A nurturing, open fellowship of believers can do much to help the

wounded. But when symptoms continue, one needs to seek the assistance of a professional counselor. If you believe that any possibility of a biological basis exists, be sure to see someone who can diagnose and treat such a problem. There are different types of psychotherapy; some problems respond better to one type than to another. Therapists have their biases and generally lean toward one or more types of therapy over the others. So seek a therapist carefully.

There Is Hope

With the tremendous recent advances in treating virtually all types of emotional problems, I can honestly point out reasons to be optimistic about improvement. Definite progress is being made in determining the specific type of therapy most helpful for a given illness. The medical field strides forward every year with greater understanding of the biology of these diseases and with new medications. I am not saying that there are quick fixes or 100 percent cures, but today's treatments completely surpass those available in years past. We must be patient, though: I have patients who did poorly until we tried the sixth or seventh combination of medications, after which we saw marked improvement.

I see even greater reason for hope when, in addition to the medical profession, patients and their families do their part. Also, as the church becomes more understanding and accepting of emotional illness, we will progress still further in assisting the wounded among us.

Let me illustrate the reason for hope with one illness—schizophrenia—which has the reputation of carrying the worst prognosis of all mental illnesses. A general practitioner in a rural area of England, C. A. H. Watts, kept records on seventy-three schizophrenia patients during his twenty-eight-year practice. During the first ten years of his retirement, he tracked down the patients he had treated. Of those he could trace, 28 percent had made a "complete recovery" and another 27 percent had only "minimal disablement."[3] In 1946, when Watts began his practice, most schizophrenics spent their lives in mental institutions; by 1983, when he completed his study, 55 percent of his former patients were able to lead normal lives.

In the early 1950s, the now-famous Vermont Longitudinal Study began to follow the progress of 269 of the most "hopeless" schizophrenic patients. Each had been hospitalized one to ten times, with an average continuous hospitalization of six years, and an average sixteen years of illness and ten years of disability. They were placed in a rehabilitation program, treated with medications, and assisted with support and reintegration into their home communities as soon as possible. Thirty-two years later, the study described one-half to two-thirds of these individuals as improved or recovered. Twenty-six percent were employed. Moreover, these findings are consistent with five other studies throughout the world.[4]

These studies followed the *sickest* patients. Most of the people I see have other disorders with a much better prognosis. They hold down professional or other highly responsible jobs and lead very productive lives as individuals and as Christians. In fact, a recent report prepared by the Advisory Council to the National Institute of Mental Health has verified, through controlled clinical studies, that the success rate in treating our most severe mental disorders is very effective. From 75 to 80 percent of all individuals with manic-depressive illness live essentially normal lives. Without treatment, these people would spend one-fourth of their lives in the hospital and half of their lives disabled.

From 65 to 85 percent of persons with major depression are treated successfully. Eighty percent of those with panic disorder are effectively treated, and for obsessive-compulsive disorder and schizophrenia it's 60 percent. This compares extremely favorably with many other "physical" disorders. For example, surgery to open up a clogged vessel (angioplasty) of a patient with heart disease is only 41 percent successful.[5]

God Will Use You

A wife of a seminary student came to see me; she had a history of bulimia and was struggling with depression. Because she knew I had served on numerous pastoral search committees, she tearfully asked if her illness would keep her husband from getting a pastorate. If I knew about her struggles, would I then vote against her husband? I answered: "No! As long as you are dealing with the problems—doing what you can, and accepting what you can't change—I believe God can use you and your husband in the ministry."

In fact, if you have weaknesses and have honestly faced them—note that I don't say "eradicated them"—you have an asset! Hebrews 5:2 tells us that the one who is "beset with weakness" is able to help others with difficulties. You possess the prerequisite to give special empathy and assistance to many who are struggling.

In 2 Corinthians 4, Paul describes his struggles and proclaims that he preaches not himself, but only Christ. He illustrates his point by calling our human bodies earthen vessels (v. 7). These vessels aren't ornamental; they don't sparkle and attract attention. They are made of clay—"fallible and fragile but functional."[6] According to Romans 9:21, one vessel may have more honor than another; but, as we see in 2 Corinthians, what really matters is the treasure within the vessel—Christ. Later Paul writes:

> And He has said to me, "My grace is sufficient for you, for power is perfected in weakness." Most gladly, therefore, I will rather boast about my weaknesses, that the power of Christ may dwell in me. Therefore I am well content with weakness, . . . distresses, . . . difficulties, for Christ's sake; for when I am weak, then I am strong. (2 Cor 12:9-10)

You *Can* Meet God's Aspirations

God doesn't grade on a curve. He knows where each one of us is in our spiritual and emotional growth, and he aspires for us only what we are capable of achieving. But God does want us to use the talent we do have, regardless of how it compares with the talents of other people.

God gives some people five talents, others two and still others one (Mt 25:14-30). I believe God has blessed me with about three talents. If I'm satisfied with only one talent, I will miss God's best for me. On the other hand, if I demand five I lay an impossible load on myself.

Maybe God has entrusted you with two emotional talents. But if you and other individuals demand that you put out more than two talents' worth of performance, it will create tremendous emotional burdens for you. These burdens, which God longs to lift with his grace, can even prevent you from doing the two talents' worth you are able to do. Some people tend to expect more of themselves and of others than God does; they need to soften and adjust their harsh expectations.

Our heavenly Father is not a "hard man," as the individual given the one talent thought. So take heart! Whatever your ability, you can please God!

First Corinthians 9:24 says, "Do you not know that those who run in a race all run, but only one receives the prize? Run in such a way that you may win." Paul is not saying that only one super-Christian can win the race and all the rest will lose. Nor is he saying that only one person per church can come in first. He is instructing each of us to run our own individual race in such a way as to win. In God's eyes we can each win our race, because he knows the capabilities of each one.

A certain man who has severe schizophrenia illustrates this point. He and his family have struggled with the "whys" of having such a disease incapacitate him for decades. Though unable to hold a job or do much else in the eyes of the world, he has faithfully given himself, on a daily basis, to intercessory prayer. I believe he is using his one talent faithfully. Isn't his situation reminiscent of the poor widow who gave her mere penny? Jesus commended her (Mk 12:41-44). So too will this dedicated Christian with schizophrenia receive God's commendation: "Well done, good and faithful servant; . . . enter thou into the joy of thy lord" (Mt 25:23 KJV).

The Shepherd's Tender Love

We need to keep in mind that God, as the Good Shepherd, does not stand at the door scolding the sheep for their bruises, ticks and ignorance, or for wandering off and getting lost. He welcomes his sheep, protects them and soothes their wounds with oil. You are his sheep, and he knows you by name; he loves and cares for you. As Jeremiah 31:3 says, he loves you with an everlasting love and draws you to him with lovingkindness.

Appendix

Are Drugs of the Devil or Tools for Healing?

Many people seem caught up by a powerful undercurrent of fear regarding medications for emotional illnesses. Especially among Christians, people often fear psychiatrists because they have been stereotyped as "drug-happy"—ready to prescribe excessive amounts of medication that aren't always needed.

Whether drugs are helpful, whether they are necessary, and whether psychiatrists are "drug-happy" are all legitimate questions which the appendix seeks to answer.

Are All Psychiatrists Drug-Happy?

Not long ago I read a letter in the *Psychiatry Section Newsletter* of the Christian Medical & Dental Society (CMDS). The writer had "a bone to pick" on behalf of psychiatric patients on medications. He expressed a concern that many people feel. The letter writer referred to a presentation he made before a number of psychiatrists on the theme of "stigma."

I made the generalization that *"all healing comes from God"* whether it is through the instrument of a believing or atheistic surgeon or psychiatrist.

Then I talked about believers who have a strong fear of drugs and resent being sustained on strong medication over a long period of time by a Christian psychiatrist. I said that I thought doctors expelled those fears too much. The natural fears patients have of psychiatrists are directed toward medication, mystery, and manipulation. . . .

The bone of contention I have is that I sensed no-one listened to what I said about excessive medication of patients. . . .

Are doctors brainwashed today in terms of drugs? Is it good treatment procedure to use an excessive amount of medication on a patient who wants to exercise more self-control? Is it moral to prescribe a legal drug when it is unnecessary, harmful, or disturbing to the patient? Where are the lines drawn?

Over and over I'm hearing people relate that they seek out a Christian psychiatrist because the unbelieving doctor they have been seeing is not helping them but keeps them on medications. They call CMDS for recommendation of a Christian psychiatrist who will not string them out on drugs. Occasionally they reject a name of a CMDS member because they have already found he/she force-feeds medication in the same way as anyone else.

This is not an ax I'm grinding. . . . Am I naive to believe what patients tell me? Can it be that Christian psychiatrists only rarely err in this regard? Or is this something you practice without being aware of violating your patient's native fear of being out of control or overly dependent on drugs? . . .

No-one discussed this after my talk. I have a stigma against drug-happy psychiatrists. And if *I* am bothered by this, what about the hundreds of other Christian workers and patients out there who share my concern? The thing that bothers me today is my uneasiness that it doesn't seem to bother you. Will you respond and let's get this out on the table with some enlightening discussion?

I invite responses for this *Psychiatry Section Newsletter.* I will be even more disturbed if no-one has anything to say.

Sid Macaulay

Staff assigned to CMDS Psychiatry Section[1]

I remember reading this letter and slouching down in my chair in resigned frustration, thinking, *He has not walked in my moccasins.* He has never had a paranoid patient come after him with an ax or had a distraught family member call because a loved one is ready to take her life—and know that medications would have prevented these crises.

I thought of a certain patient whom a minister referred to me. At the beginning of his appointment, the patient laid out the ground rules: he would talk to me and let me pray with him, but under no circumstance would he take any medications. My initial evaluation clearly demonstrated that he was a very paranoid and psychotic individual. So after that evaluation I prayed with him and told him that under his requirements I couldn't help him further. The next day he returned, demanding to exorcise the devil from me. Two days later he stormed into my waiting room with a Bible in one hand and pounded on my office door with an ax in the other hand. He charged around, threatening my life and terrifying everyone in the office until police arrived to take him to a hospital.

Why Do We React So Strongly Against Medications?
I seriously questioned whether it would be of any use to write a reply to Sid Macaulay's letter. *If he's already made up his mind, nothing I could say would change it. So what's the use?* I thought. But the clincher for me was his statement "I will be even more disturbed if no-one has anything to say." Since I had no idea whether any of my colleagues would write, I did reply. The ideas in this chapter grow out of the letter I sent in response. But again, I sometimes wonder if people can "hear" what I have to say when many people have such strong emotional reactions to any mention of medications for emotional problems.

Part of the problem, I believe, is all the stigma associated with the treatment of mental patients. Outdated methods and past abuses, real or exaggerated, have left an indelible impression on our society. Movies such as *One Flew over the Cuckoo's Nest* have stereotyped psychiatric staff as villains who inflict cruel "treatments," and they have depicted patients who resist as courageous heroes. In addition, medications like Valium received a lot of negative press in the seventies. Some of it was appropriate, some probably not—but we still live under its influence.

In response to my lengthy letter, Sid wrote in part:
Thank you so much for your excellent letter. . . . It is very helpful to me. . . . I am growing confident that there are real misunderstandings about the nature of drugs and the way they are used. . . . I certainly hope that the stigma can be turned around. . . . There is a lack of effective education . . . with regard to the way psychiatrists treat and make use of helpful medications.

I feel the general public, including believers in the Church, are unaware of the way . . . quality of life is [improved] by a willingness to be on medication for those who are disturbed.

In the rest of this chapter I will cover some of the major items that I covered in my letter to Sid.

When Do Drugs Make Sense?
It is extremely difficult, if not impossible, to treat the psychotic, depressed, suicidal, manic-depressive or extremely anxious patient without the assistance of medications. Patients with these kinds of difficulties often come to a doctor and insist, "Get me better without medications." A diabetic would never go into

an emergency room in a crisis and request treatment but demand that insulin not be used. The man with the ax is an extreme example of one who refuses to take any medication yet needs it desperately. In a situation like this doctors are sued for malpractice if they don't use medications.

Admittedly, most patients are not in the desperate condition of the patient with the ax. Who then does and does not need medications? I can divide the patients I see into four categories.

In the first group are those struggling with emotional/spiritual issues that would be inappropriate to treat with medications. I don't prescribe any for these patients.

The second group consists of those whose issues cause enough distressing symptoms that medications might significantly help them. Medications are a serious possibility but not mandatory. With these individuals I discuss frankly my reasons for considering medications, the benefits and potential risks. Then together we decide whether or not to use medications.

The third group of individuals have significant problems functioning and may, for example, have persisting serious, suicidal thoughts. To such I firmly and strongly recommend medications. Most of them accept my recommendations—but for those who don't, I use all the other means at my disposal, without medications.

The last category of patients have such serious difficulty that to treat them without medications would put them and myself at an unacceptably high risk for some catastrophic consequence. I give these persons the choice of continuing under my care and taking the medication or discontinuing therapy with me and seeking it from someone else. The man who came after me with the ax and Bible fits into this category. In the last seventeen years that I have practiced psychiatry, only about six persons have had to choose between seeing me and taking medication or discontinuing therapy with me.

Mary, described in the first chapter, came to me with severe depression. She would fit somewhere between the second and third categories, so I initially tried to treat her without any medications. However, her feelings were so overwhelming and her thinking so muddled that it kept her from making any progress at all. So I recommended an antidepressant along with the therapy while we worked on many of the factors contributing to her depression.

It took about a month for her to feel better. As she dealt with issues in her life, we were able to reduce her medications by one-third. But the symptoms and issues that remained, plus the strong family history that suggested a biological basis for her illness, made me reluctant to decrease her medications too quickly.

About this time, four months after she had initially come to see me, a friend said to her, "Aren't you over that yet? You're still taking drugs? You know, you're going to get hooked on them!" Her husband also remained skeptical about her seeing a psychiatrist and "taking pills." So Mary called me to say she was doing so well that she wanted to stop therapy and medications. I agreed that she was doing much better, but cautioned her about abruptly stopping her therapy and medications—to no avail.

Six weeks later I received a call from the emergency room. Mary had taken a lethal dose of aspirin. Fortunately, someone got to her in time. After three days in intensive care she was finally alert, but very depressed. After a month's stay in the hospital, during which she resumed the antidepressants, she could return home, but she still functioned marginally. It took another six months of outpatient therapy for her to get back to the level where she had been before discontinuing her medications.

When people are in a severe crisis, it may take weeks to help them become emotionally stabilized with the help of medications. Then they often feel so well that they want to discontinue the medication immediately. We physicians may have a very good idea, based on experience and research, of the likelihood of their continuing to function well without the medication. When we believe there is a high probability of a recurrence, we are reluctant to discontinue the medication.

Mary's story is typical. Too many times after patients discontinue medications—when we recommended they not—we get called at 3:00 a.m. by the patient, a relative or a friend complaining, "Why don't you do something?" Often such repeat crises in some way jeopardize the lives of the patients and others around them. Also, it often takes weeks for the medications to become effective again.

In the free societies of the West, virtually any patient may choose to refuse medication.[2] In addition, a person is always free to seek a second opinion or to transfer to a psychologist, an MFCC (marriage, family and child counselor), a licensed social worker or a lay counselor who can't prescribe medications. If patients fall into the third or fourth category described above, however, their treatment probably cannot be the most effective without the assistance of medications.

I allow my patients the freedom to refuse medications, and I agree that this freedom is important. But it's also extremely important that Christian leaders develop a greater appreciation for the gravity of emotional illnesses. They need to appreciate the fact that up to 15 percent of our population at any one time has significant emotional problems. These are bona fide illnesses, many with a biological basis, and some victims desperately need medications.

Mary's story illustrates the consequences for the Christian who resists not only therapy but also medications. I am reminded of the fact that it was Christians who opposed the use of ether for anesthesia during childbirth or surgery when it first became available. They reasoned right out of Genesis that if God didn't want people to have pain he wouldn't have given women pain in childbirth. Therefore such a drug shouldn't be used—on a scriptural basis. Few would hold to such reasoning about anesthesia today, but we hold to similar logic about medications for mental illness.

Recent Breakthroughs and New Lives

As discussed in chapters four and five, distinct, measurable chemical changes appear with many types of emotional problems. The key to these widespread changes seems to be twenty or more different neurotransmitters that interconnect the brain cells (neurons) with each another. Years ago we did not understand these changes, so our treatments were crude.

A century ago doctors treated all kinds of problems with a few general means—sort of a shotgun approach. Bloodletting was the treatment of choice for a wide variety of ailments. Now blood is removed from a person for only one or two specific illnesses—conditions for which this treatment has proved to help. We have learned how to treat other problems with other means. Likewise, half a century ago psychiatry was at a primitive "all-purpose-bloodletting-stage-of-knowledge" in our use of medications that affect the mind (psychotropic medications). Everyone got phenobarbital or chloral hydrate, with only marginal help.

Now our vast increase in knowledge about the brain is leading to new medications every year. These allow the physician to pinpoint the chemical problem more precisely and often to remedy it. We can now treat many symptoms more accurately than ever before.

Out of the Institution

The first major breakthrough with medications came in 1954, with the discovery of major tranquilizers. Patients with psychotic symptoms like hallucinations, delusions and paranoia seem to have an overactive dopamine neurotransmitter system; major tranquilizers interfere with the transmission of dopamine, restoring it to a more normal level. With this group of medications tens of thousands of patients were able to be discharged from state mental hospitals.

One of my patients, who has had severe emotional problems for over twenty-five years and who has spent more than two years altogether in psychiatric hospitals even with medications, said to me, "If it weren't for these medications I probably would have spent most of my adult life in a mental institution and would have lost my husband and daughter." Another patient with a severe emotional illness recently said, "If it weren't for these medications, I'd be six feet under."

In all probability, if you attend a church of more than a hundred, at least one person there functions as a normal member of society only because of these medications. Before 1954 this person would have resided in a mental institution.[3]

Awake and Alive

While certain neurotransmitter chemicals are increased in psychotic individuals, they are decreased with depression.

We now possess a variety of antidepressant medications to restore these to normal levels. As with all medicine, sometimes we have to try several medications until we find the right one for a given person. But when we discover the right one, I see the individual—as I've seen numerous patients—improve dramatically.

Here I am reminded of Jake, a missionary who suffered his entire adult life from insomnia. He had trouble going to sleep and slept fitfully after 3:00 a.m. for years. Not infrequently his wife would see the light on in the wee hours of the morning, because Jake knew he was wasting his time staying in bed. His low energy level and mild depression greatly decreased his productivity. A very small dose of an antidepressant resolved these symptoms and markedly improved his entire outlook on life and his ability to function. His wife continues to be astounded at the change in him; she even sleeps better herself, since he no longer paces the floor at night. His fellow missionaries have commented that he no longer falls asleep during meetings. And he says, "I don't have to push myself all day long to get anything done."

Quality of Life

Jackie, a "Spirit-filled" women's leader and Sunday-school teacher, had anxiety in the daytime and was often wakened in the middle of the night by panic attacks. These symptoms had plagued her since her early twenties. She has had Christians pray for her and has faithfully applied the Scriptures to her life—including everything it teaches on anxiety. Eventually she sought psychotherapy, which helped her somewhat. Then a few years ago I started her on a medication that has eradicated the attacks. Since then she has tried to discontinue the medicine many times—only to have her symptoms return. In the process she tells me she has discovered two types of anxiety. One is caused by violating Scripture—and is remedied by proper application of the Scriptures. She has this anxiety on or off the medications. The other anxiety is not related to sin; it is at best partially helped by applying scriptural principles—and is eradicated by medications.

Jackie, like Jake and many other patients, don't *have* to have medications. They will never come after me with an ax and will probably never be seriously suicidal—but their quality of life and their productivity are markedly affected by the disorders they suffer.

If you were in my shoes, would you prescribe medications for the Jackies and Jakes in your practice? Would you want to take medications if you could be helped like Jackie or Jake? Would you tell your Christian friends you are taking medications—or, like this missionary and women's leader, would you keep it to yourself for fear of being misunderstood?

Medications and Personal Responsibility

I hope that by now you can see that chemical changes—not wrong thinking or actions—are often the primary cause of emotional problems. However, one's own personal responsibility still plays a role, and one's choices sometimes make a very significant contribution to one's condition. Remember Vic in chapter seven? If he could give up the rage over his son's death, I don't think he would need medication. But for now, it's probably keeping him from committing suicide.

If we could accurately determine when the problem is due primarily to personal choice, should we refuse to treat that person with medications? In my opinion, not necessarily. I think that withholding the help "meds" can offer is like refusing to throw a rope to a person who falls into a hole and saying, "You got yourself in there. Now get yourself out."

Some individuals are trapped in such an emotional hole that it is next to impossible for them to think objectively in order to work through their problems. Yes, some have made choices that led to their falling in the hole; but without help they simply cannot get out—at least not for a very long time. In fact, their actions often tend to dig the hole deeper or cause it to cave in on them.

For such people, medication can be a rope to help them climb out of the hole. I think of one dedicated Christian who was depressed and repeatedly struggled with the question "Am I saved?" Despite the best efforts of ministers and my counseling, the question continued to haunt him, along with his ongoing depression. After an adequate dose of medication he could positively resolve the question. I continued to work with him for another year until we tapered off and eventually discontinued all his medications without a recurrence of his symptoms. I'm pleased to say he has remained assured of his salvation!

Another frequent objection to medication is that it will keep people from working on their problems or it will mask the real issue. But if a person is drowning you don't stand on the shore and give swimming lessons—you throw out a life-ring. The lessons can come later. Depression, panic and other forms of emotional turmoil are sucking many people under so they can't think straight. They need a life-preserver.

When people are severely distressed, the proper dose and type of medication actually facilitates their working through problems. Studies have shown that the thinking processes of depressed patients, for example, are severely impaired. Treatment with appropriate medication enables them to reason more like a healthy individual.[4]

I sometimes explain to patients that medications can serve the same purpose as a cast on a broken leg. The cast allows healing so that gradually more weight can be placed on the broken leg until it is strong enough for the cast to be removed. Likewise, when someone's life has been shattered, medications can help stabilize him or her until sufficient healing and growth have taken place for the person to stand on his or her own "emotional two feet." Then the medicines can be reduced. It is a great joy to see a patient improve enough to reduce the meds and even to discontinue them if there are no remissions.

What If the Patient Needs a Wheelchair?

Some make the accusation "You are going to get 'hooked' if you take drugs." But most of the medications used in this field don't cause physical dependence. It is true that a small percentage of patients will need medications for the rest of their lives, and many of them struggle with this reality. For them, accepting their condition and need can be a giant hurdle—even as the paraplegic must accept his wheelchair or the diabetic her insulin and regimented diet.

Most of us can't imagine accusing the insulin-dependent diabetic with questions such as "Are you still taking that drug? When are you going to get off of it? Are you hooked on it? Are you seeing a good doctor?" But families, friends and patients themselves commonly fire such questions at the one with emotional problems who needs medication. They show either a lack of knowledge or an inability to accept the fact that some people need medications for long periods of time in order to correct the neurotransmitter imbalance in their brains.

Today Western countries are finally beginning to allow the physically challenged to integrate into society. We provide more handicapped parking, seating, restrooms, and access to public places and transportation. We see more wheelchairs in schools, workplaces and amusement parks, and even on television. We are beginning to accept those dependent on wheelchairs as equally valuable people, not at fault for their disabilities. In the same way we must begin to accept persons who need medications if they are to get about and function in society, the workplace and the church.

How Do You Define *Necessary?*

Sid Macaulay wrote about using "excessive amount[s] of medication . . . when it is unnecessary, harmful, or disturbing to the patient." All psychiatrists would agree that medications should not be used when they are unnecessary. But "necessary" is a judgment call. If a patient with agoraphobia hasn't left her house for three years because of panic attacks, is it necessary or unnecessary to give her relief with medications, some of which are addicting? She can live without the medication—but it's not much of a life.

A few years ago I cared for a patient, an extremely dedicated Christian, who had agoraphobia and panic attacks. Not only did her condition keep her completely housebound, but she literally would not flush a toilet or turn off a light switch for fear of triggering a panic attack. (She would leave the lights on all day and wait for a family member to flush the toilet.) If you were the doctor, what would you do? Would you let her suffer or give her an addictive medication restoring her to a more normal life?

Though she was reluctant to take any "drugs," with my encouragement—after many, many months—she conceded. Eventually she went back to working full time and living a more normal life. It is true that many of the medications we use do have side effects, and some of them trouble the patient mildly to moderately. For example, a psychotic patient may complain that being on the meds "feels like being in a mental straitjacket." But one of my patients—who is able to live at home and hold down a part-time job when on the medications— would be institutionalized and possibly become suicidal or violent toward others without them.

In all branches of medicine physicians have to use medications with side effects. That's why they are obtainable by prescription only—to treat a problem that is more distressing or threatening than the possible risks. Often we must choose between mild side effects on the one hand versus the patient's incapacitating emotional distress, inability to work, and possible suicide or homicide on the other hand.

Some medications—especially the major tranquilizers—can be harmful; but so can many widely prescribed medications such as penicillin, used to fight infections, and digitalis, used for heart disease. Medications with the greater potential for dangerous side effects must not be given for trivial reasons. The patients for whom I prescribe medications have such serious problems that the help medications can offer far outweighs the possibility of harmful side effects.

With patients who desperately need medications, conscientious psychiatrists labor over these issues. We try to weigh all the medical, social, legal and quality-of-life factors in our efforts to make only appropriate use of medications.

Addiction: Problem, Prejudice and Controversy

As stated earlier, most medications used for emotional illnesses do not cause physical dependency. But there is one group of medications that can. Addiction can and does take place with the use of benzodiazepines in high doses over long periods of time. Sometimes used as sleeping pills, these meds are the "minor tranquilizers" such as Xanax, Valium, Ativan, Klonopin and Dalmane.

Controversy abounds both within and outside the medical profession regarding the appropriate use of these medications. During the 1960s Valium became extremely popular and was used effectively to treat a number of disorders: not only anxiety but also muscle spasms and convulsions. But after the Kennedy hearings (which were critical of the use of tranquilizers) and the tremendous media attention on the abuses of Valium, I, like many other physicians, limited my prescriptions of this class of medications. Subsequently, however, some patients who had been functioning fairly well experienced a marked decrease in the quality of their lives; many became unable to leave their homes or keep their jobs.

These observations, along with more recent research showing a chemical basis for some of the anxiety-related diseases, have caused me to reevaluate. I now believe it's legitimate to give a minor tranquilizer to someone such as the woman I described earlier who was unable to leave her house without it.

Jonathan Davidson of Duke University has shown, as a matter of fact, that patients with panic disorder and agoraphobia (the ones most prone to need these medications) do *not* develop an increased tolerance to the medication. Thus the dose of these medications can actually be decreased in time.[5] Other studies suggest that misuse is probably less than many believe. Yet the prejudice against benzodiazepines still keeps many people who need them from utilizing them.[6]

Because of the controversy over the use or misuse of benzodiazepines, the American Psychiatric Association established a task force to evaluate this problem and establish some guidelines. Its members concluded that two groups legitimately warrant the use of minor tranquilizers: older patients suffering with medical problems and significant anxiety, and patients with panic attacks or agoraphobia. They further concluded that the benefits clearly outweighed the risk of addiction and that it is appropriate to use these medications on a long-term basis. Controversy still surrounds their use for individuals with chronic anxiety, depression or sleep disorders.[7]

*   *   *

I believe more major breakthroughs will be made and more effective and specific medications will become available to help those who suffer with emotional symptoms. It is sad when the church heaps "guilt trips" on any of its members who need these medications, or when it tries to talk them out of taking them.

In an earlier chapter I indicated that 15 percent of the total population have significant emotional problems at any one time. Out of these, probably only one-to two-thirds need medication. In other words, 90 to 95 percent of the population *don't* need it. My plea is for full acceptance of those people who so urgently need the assistance of medication—especially the 5 to 10 percent in your congregation.

I want to close with a little story that depicts the situation of many people. A woman was alone in her house during a flood. She prayed that God would spare her life. Some men came along in a four-wheel-drive vehicle and urged her to come with them to shelter. She declined, saying, "God will rescue me." It kept raining until the water came up the front porch. She continued to pray.

Soon some other men came along in a rowboat and urged her to come with them. Again she insisted, "God will rescue me."

Before long the water flooded her house. Forced to perch on the roof with her pets at her side, she pleaded with God for deliverance. A helicopter came along and threw her a rope, which she refused.

The woman and her pets drowned. When she got to heaven, she asked God why he didn't rescue her. He said, "I sent you a man in a four-wheel-drive, two men in a rowboat and even a helicopter—and you refused all those efforts. What more did you want?"

Maybe God *is* sending us help—but sometimes the vehicle he uses isn't what we had in mind!

Notes

Chapter 1: Don't Shoot! I'm Already Wounded!

[1] Charles R. Solomon, *Handbook of Happiness* (Denver: Grace Fellowship Press, 1971), p. 48.

[2] Michael Harper, *Spiritual Warfare: Recognizing and Overcoming the Work of Evil Spirits* (Ann Arbor, Mich.: Servant, 1984), p. 82.

[3] Dwight J. Pentecost, *Man's Problems—God's Answers* (Chicago: Moody Press, 1974), p. 52.

[4] Dave Hunt, *Beyond Seduction: A Return to Biblical Christianity* (Eugene, Ore.: Harvest House, 1987), pp. 114, 127.

[5] John F. MacArthur Jr., *Our Sufficiency in Christ: Three Deadly Influences That Undermine Your Spiritual Life* (Dallas: Word, 1991), pp. 58, 77, 89.

[6] "Public Perception of Mental Illness," 1988 survey and report from the National Alliance for the Mentally Ill, *The Psychiatric Times*, September 1990, p. 80.

[7] "The Stigma of Mental Illness," Publication 90-1470, National Institute of Mental Health, U.S. Department of Health & Human Services.

[8] A. Silk, "Is It Fair to Blame the Victim?" Correspondence, *The Western Journal of Medicine* 152 (1990): 186-87.

[9] Hunt, *Beyond Seduction*, pp. 114, 127.

Chapter 2: Why We Wound

[1] Personal correspondence from Harold J. Sala of Guidelines International Ministries.

[2] "Psychiatrists Typically Encounter One Patient Suicide During Each Eight Years of Practice," *Clinical Psychiatric News*, December 1990.

[3] Earl S. Johnson Jr., "What to Wear When You're Depressed," *Eternity*, Decem-

ber 1976, p. 20.

[4]K. B. Wells et al., "The Functioning and Well-Being of Depressed Patients: Results from the Medical Outcomes Study," *Journal of the American Medical Association,* August 18, 1989, pp. 914-19.

[5]"The Stigma of Mental Illness," U.S. Department of Health & Human Services.

[6]Dwight Carlson and Susan Carlson Wood, *When Life Isn't Fair* (Eugene, Ore.: Harvest House, 1989).

[7]Abraham Lincoln, source unknown.

[8]Tim LaHaye, *How to Win over Depression* (Grand Rapids, Mich.: Zondervan, 1974), p. 99.

[9]Hunt, *Beyond Seduction,* p. 114.

Chapter 3: Can a Spirit-Filled Christian Have Emotional Problems?

[1]Carlson and Wood, *When Life Isn't Fair,* p. 33.

[2]MacArthur, *Our Sufficiency in Christ,* pp. 18-19.

[3]Ibid., pp. 53, 58.

[4]Ibid., pp. 57, 66, 107-8.

[5]Quoted in Roland H. Bainton, *Here I Stand: A Life of Martin Luther* (Nashville: Abingdon, 1950), pp. 361, 28 and again 361.

[6]Richard E. Day, *The Shadow of the Broad Brim* (Philadelphia: Judson Press, 1934), pp. 97, 68, 76, 177.

[7]Quoted in Warren W. Wiersbe, "Insight for the Pastor: Discouragement—an Occupational Hazard," *Moody Monthly,* September 1974, p. 67.

[8]Quoted in Day, *Shadow of the Broad Brim,* p. 177.

[9]Ray Cripps, "Dark Night of the Soul," *Guideposts,* February 1967; Vera Phillips and Edwin Robertson, *J. B. Phillips: The Wounded Healer* (Grand Rapids, Mich.: Eerdmans, 1984); J. B. Phillips, *Your God Is Too Small* (New York: Macmillan, 1957), p. 51.

[10]Gerald F. Hawthorne, *Philippians,* Word Biblical Commentary 43 (Waco, Tex.: Word, 1983), p. 110.

[11]For a complete scriptural study on the appropriate and inappropriate place of anger, see my book *Overcoming Hurts and Anger* (Eugene, Ore.: Harvest House, 1981).

[12]Hawthorne, *Philippians,* p. 183.

[13]W. E. Vine, *An Expository Dictionary of New Testament Words* (Old Tappan, N.J.: Revell, 1966), 1:30, 208; 2:70, 224; 4:95, 174, 198.

[14]Charles A. Wanamaker, *The Epistles to the Thessalonians* (Grand Rapids, Mich.:

Eerdmans, 1990), p. 198; David Black, "The Weak in Thessalonica: A Study in Pauline Lexicography," *Journal of the Evangelical Theological Society,* September 1982, pp. 307-21.

[15]Ernest Best, *A Commentary on the First and Second Epistles to the Thessalonians* (New York: Harper & Row, 1972), pp. 229-33.

[16]Jim Morud, "Christians on the Couch," *Moody Monthly,* May 1991, pp. 14-15.

[17]C. S. Lewis, *The Problem of Pain* (New York: Macmillan, 1961), p. 70.

[18]A. W. Tozer, *The Knowledge of the Holy* (New York: Harper & Brothers, 1961), p. 110.

[19]For a more detailed scriptural development of this subject, see Carlson and Wood, *When Life Isn't Fair,* chapters 5-6.

[20]Lewis L. Judd, "Decade of the Brain: Implications for Clinical Psychiatric Practice," lecture given at the California Psychiatric Association 1991 annual meeting, October 13, 1991.

Chapter 4: It's Not Necessarily "All in Your Mind"

[1]World Health Organization, *The International Classification of Diseases: Ninth Revision Clinical Modification* (Washington, D.C.: U.S. Department of Health and Human Services, 1980).

[2]Darrel A. Regier et al., "One-Month Prevalence of Mental Disorders in the United States," *Archives of General Psychiatry* 45 (1988): 977-86; "Who Needs Psychiatric Help?" (Washington, D.C.: American Psychiatric Association Press, n.d.).

To help you understand the various levels of emotional illness more clearly, let's compare an emotional illness with a physical illness such as a duodenal ulcer. There are many people who suffer from indigestion. However, evaluation by a medical doctor would show that though many have uncomfortable symptoms, only some actually have a full-fledged duodenal ulcer. The latter would warrant the diagnosis of such an illness. A few would have such severe symptoms (possibly a bleeding ulcer) that hospitalization would be required. The same is true for an emotional disorder. Not everyone with symptoms of anxiety, obsession or depression would meet the diagnostic criteria for a given mental illness. Of those who do, some would have more severe symptoms than others and at times would need hospitalization.

The figures that I quote throughout the book on the incidence of various illnesses are *averages* from the literature. And since some people have more than one emotional illness during their lifetime, multiple occurrences are also taken into consideration.

[3]A. E. Bergin, "Religiosity and Mental Health: A Critical Reevaluation and Meta-analysis," *Professional Psychology: Research and Practice* 14, no. 2 (1983): 170-84.

[4]William Glasser, *Reality Therapy: A New Approach to Psychiatry* (New York: Harper & Row, 1965); Leonard Zusne, *Names in the History of Psychology: A Biographical Sourcebook* (Washington, D.C.: Hemisphere, 1975), p. 127.

[5]Mandel E. Cohen and Paul D. White, "Life Situations, Emotions and Neurocirculatory Asthenia (Anxiety Neurosis, Neurasthenia, Effort Syndrome)," *Association for Research on Nervous and Mental Diseases Proceedings* 29 (1950): 832-69; B. S. Oppenheimer and M. A. Rothschild, "The Psychoneurotic Factor in the Irritable Heart of Soldiers," *Journal of the American Medical Association* 70, no. 25 (1918): 1919-23.

[6]Howard Fishman, "Panic Disorder and Treatment Decisions: Beyond the Short Term," *Advances in Psychiatric Medicine*, August 1990, pp. 45-50; "Better Outcomes in Panic Disorder," *Advances in Psychiatric Medicine*, January 1989 (supp.), pp. 1-8.

[7]Raymond R. Crowe, "The Genetics of Panic Disorder and Agoraphobia," *Psychiatric Developments* 2 (1985): 171-86.

[8]Ferris N. Pitts Jr. and James N. McClure Jr., "Lactate Metabolism in Anxiety Neurosis," *The New England Journal of Medicine* 277, no. 25 (1967): 1329-36.

[9]M. Mellersh Jones V, "Comparison of Exercise Response in Anxiety States and Normal Controls," *Psychosomatic Medicine* 8 (1946): 180-87; David V. Sheehan, *The Anxiety Disease* (New York: Charles Scribner's Sons, 1983), pp. 90-95.

[10]Richard I. Shader et al., "Panic Disorders: Current Perspectives," *Journal of Clinical Psychopharmacology* (supp.) 2, no. 6 (1982): 2S-10S.

[11]Howard I. Kaplan and Benjamin J. Sadock, eds., *Comprehensive Textbook of Psychiatry*, 5th ed. (Baltimore: Williams & Wilkins, 1989), pp. 702, 863, 954; Thomas W. Uhde, "Caffeine Provocation of Panic: A Focus on Biological Mechanisms," paper presented at a conference on panic attacks, University of California—Davis, January 1990.

[12]Thomas A. Mellman and Thomas W. Uhde, "Patients with Frequent Sleep Panic: Clinical Findings and Response to Medication Treatment," *Journal of Clinical Psychiatry* 51, no. 12 (1990): 513-16.

[13]Mats Humble, "Aetiology and Mechanisms of Anxiety Disorders," *Acta Psychiatrica Scandinavia* 76, supp. 335 (1987): 15-30.

[14]Abby J. Fyer et al., "Familial Transmission of Simple Phobias and Fears,"

Archives of General Psychiatry 47 (March 1990): 252-56; Kenneth S. Kendler et al., "Generalized Anxiety Disorder in Women: A Population-Based Twin Study," *Archives of General Psychiatry* 49 (April 1992): 267-72; Kenneth S. Kendler et al., "The Genetic Epidemiology of Phobias in Women," *Archives of General Psychiatry* 49 (April 1992): 273-81; Svenn Torgersen, "Genetic Factors in Anxiety Disorders," *Archives of General Psychiatry* 40 (October 1983): 1085-92.

About 15 percent of the population will suffer some type of diagnosable anxiety disorder during their lifetime. Up to half of these people will have panic attacks. The others will have a more generalized anxiety (nervousness, uneasiness or apprehension). Genetics appears to play a role in many of these individuals with heritability estimated around 30 percent. Others have phobias such as a fear of cats or heights, and this is highly familial with close relatives having a 30 to 40 percent incidence of this disorder.

[15]G. E. Berrios, "Obsessive-Compulsive Disorder: Its Conceptual History in France During the Nineteenth Century," *Comprehensive Psychiatry* 30 (July/August 1989): 283-95.

[16]Kaplan and Sadock, *Comprehensive Textbook of Psychiatry*, p. 986.

[17]Judith L. Rapoport, *The Boy Who Couldn't Stop Washing: The Experience and Treatment of Obsessive-Compulsive Disorder* (New York: Dutton, 1989), pp. 94-96; Susan E. Swedo et al., "High Prevalence of Obsessive-Compulsive Symptoms in Patients with Sydenham's Chorea," *American Journal of Psychiatry* 146, no. 2 (1989): 246-49.

[18]Lewis R. Baxter Jr. et al., "PET Imaging in Obsessive Compulsive Disorder with and Without Depression," *Journal of Clinical Psychiatry* 51 supp. (April 1990): 61-70.

[19]Godfrey D. Pearlson, "Medication Found to Ease Brain Blood Flow Abnormality in OCD," *Clinical Psychiatric News* 19, no. 5 (1991); Judith L. Rapoport, "The Biology of Obsessions and Compulsions," *Scientific American*, March 1989, pp. 82-89.

[20]Ibid.

[21]Steven A. Rasmussen and Jane L. Eisen, "Epidemiology of Obsessive Compulsive Disorder," *Journal of Clinical Psychiatry* 51 supp. (August 1990): 20-23; John J. Schwab, "Obsessive-Compulsive Disorder: Part 1, An Overview," *Clinical Advances in Treatment of Psychiatric Disorders* 4 (July/August 1990).

[22]Howard Fishman, ed., "Recent Advances in Obsessive-Compulsive Disorder," *The Psychiatric Times*, September 1990 (supp.), pp. 1-4.

[23]Nancy L. Segal et al., "Tourette's Disorder in a Set of Reared-Apart Triplets: Genetic and Environmental Influences," *American Journal of Psychiatry* 147, no. 2 (1990): 196-99.

[24]Brian A. Fallon et al., "The Pharmacotherapy of Moral or Religious Scrupulosity," *Journal of Clinical Psychiatry* 51, no. 12 (1990): 517-21; S. Swedo, "A Double Blind Comparison of Clompiramine and Desipramine in the Treatment of Trichotillomania (Hair Pulling)," *New England Journal of Medicine* 321, no. 8 (1989): 497-501; "Trichotillomania U.S. Prevalence at 2 Percent, Experts Report Data at National Conference," *The Psychiatric Times*, December 1992, pp. 1, 33-34.

Chapter 5: It's Not Necessarily "All in Your Mind," Continued

[1]Richard C. Shelton et al., "Cerebral Structural Pathology in Schizophrenia: Evidence for a Selective Prefrontal Cortical Defect," *American Journal of Psychiatry* 145, no. 2 (1988): 154-63.

[2]Nancy C. Andreasen et al., "Ventricular Enlargement in Schizophrenia Evaluated with Computed Tomographic Scanning," *Archives of General Psychiatry* 47 (November 1990): 1008-15.

Figures shown are similar to those that appear in many articles or books such as Kaplan and Sadock, *Comprehensive Textbook of Psychiatry*, pp. 702-8.

[3]Richard L. Suddath et al., "Temporal Lobe Pathology in Schizophrenia: A Quantitative Magnetic Resonance Imaging Study," *American Journal of Psychiatry* 146, no. 4 (1989): 464-72.

[4]Daniel R. Weinberger, "Premorbid Neuropathology in Schizophrenia," Letters to the Editor, *The Lancet*, August 20, 1988, p. 445.

[5]"Schizophrenics' Brains," *Science*, March 30, 1990, p. 1539.

[6]Steven E. Arnold et al., "Some Cytoarchitectural Abnormalities of the Entorhinal Cortex in Schizophrenia," *Archives of General Psychiatry* 48 (July 1991): 625-32; Patrick E. Barta et al., "Auditory Hallucinations and Smaller Superior Temporal Gyral Volume in Schizophrenia," *American Journal of Psychiatry* 147, no. 11 (1990): 1457-62; Dilip V. Jeste and James B. Lohr, "Hippocampal Pathologic Findings in Schizophrenia," *Archives of General Psychiatry* 46 (November 1989): 1019-24; M. D. Pakkenbert, "Pronounced Reduction of Total Neuron Number in Mediodorsal Thalamic Nucleus and Nucleus Accumbens in Schizophrenics," *Archives of General Psychiatry* 47 (November 1990): 1023-28.

[7]Andrew J. Conrad et al., "Hippocampal Pyramidal Cell Disarray in Schizophre-

nia as a Bilateral Phenomenon," *Archives of General Psychiatry* 48 (May 1991): 413-17; Andrew J. Conrad et al., "Schizophrenia and the Hippocampus: The Embryological Hypothesis Extended," *Schizophrenia Bulletin* 13, no. 4 (1987): 577-87.

[8]Elaine Walker and Richard J. Lewine, "Prediction of Adult-Onset Schizophrenia from Childhood Home Movies of the Patients," *American Journal of Psychiatry* 147 (August 1990): 1052-56; Barbara Fish et al., "Infants at Risk for Schizophrenia: Sequelae of a Genetic Neurointegrative Defect," *Archives of General Psychiatry* 49 (March 1992): 221-35.

[9]Miron Baron and Rhoda Gruen, "Risk Factors in Schizophrenia: Season of Birth and Family History," *British Journal of Psychiatry* 152 (1988): 460-565; Christopher E. Barr et al., "Exposure to Influenza Epidemics During Gestation and Adult Schizophrenia: A Forty-Year Study," *Archives of General Psychiatry* 47 (September 1990): 869-74; Robert B. Zipursky and S. Charles Schulz, "Seasonality of Birth and CT Findings in Schizophrenia," *Biological Psychiatry* 22 (1987): 1288-92.

[10]Miron Baron et al., "Modern Research Criteria and the Genetics of Schizophrenia," *American Journal of Psychiatry* 142 (June 1985): 697-701; Kenneth S. Kendler, "Overview: A Current Perspective on Twin Studies of Schizophrenia," *American Journal of Psychiatry* 140 (November 1983): 1413-25; Seymour S. Kety, "Mental Illness in the Biological and Adoptive Relatives of Schizophrenic Adoptees: Findings Relevant to Genetic and Environmental Factors in Etiology," *American Journal of Psychiatry* 140 (June 1983): 720-27.

[11]Kaplan and Sadock, *Comprehensive Textbook of Psychiatry*, p. 738; Herbert Pardes et al., "Genetics and Psychiatry: Past Discoveries, Current Dilemmas and Future Directions," *American Journal of Psychiatry* 146, no. 4 (1989): 435-43; "Study Links Genetic Defect to Schizophrenia," *The Psychiatric Times*, January 1989, p. 34; "Advances in Psychiatric Medicine," *The Psychiatric Times*, January 1989.

[12]Kenneth S. Kendler and C. Dennis Robinette, "Schizophrenia in the National Academy of Sciences-National Research Council Twin Registry: A Sixteen-Year Update," *American Journal of Psychiatry* 140 (December 1983): 1551-63; Kenneth S. Kendler and Peter Hays, "Familial and Sporadic Schizophrenia: A Symptomatic, Prognostic and EEG Comparison," *American Journal of Psychiatry* 139 (December 1982): 1557-62.

For the parent who has a child with schizophrenia, it's important to understand that there may be at least two forms of this illness: one that is hereditary and another that is sporadic, having little or no genetic basis. And even when schizophrenia is genetically influenced, the specific genetic abnormality may be produced during the reproductive process, as it is in Down syndrome. Neither the parents nor other siblings may have the genetic abnormality even when a child has a genetically influenced illness.

[13]Zusne, *Names in the History of Psychology,* pp. 205-6.

[14]H. Stefan Bracha et al., "Second-Trimester Markers of Fetal Size in Schizophrenia: A Study of Monozygotic Twins," *American Journal of Psychiatry* 149 (October 1992): 1355-61.

[15]Kenneth S. Kendler et al., "A Population-Based Twin Study of Major Depression in Women: The Impact of Varying Definitions of Illness," *Archives of General Psychiatry* 49 (April 1992): 257-66; P. McGuffin et al., "The Camberwell Collaborative Depressive Study: Part 3, Depression and Adversity in the Relatives of Depressed Probands," *British Journal of Psychiatry* 152 (1988): 775-82; Arthur D. Sorosky, ed., *The Handbook of Modern Psychopharmacology* (Reseda, Calif.: Bio-psychiatric Laboratory, 1983), p. 32.

[16]Zusne, *Names in the History of Psychology,* p. 190.

[17]Kaplan and Sadock, *Comprehensive Textbook of Psychiatry,* pp. 863-68; Elliott Richelson, "Biological Basis of Depression and Therapeutic Relevance," *Journal of Clinical Psychiatry* 52 supp. (June 1991): 4-10.

[18]Peter P. Roy-Byrne et al., "The Relationship of Menstrually Related Mood Disorders to Psychiatric Disorders," *Clinical Obstetrics and Gynecology* 30 (June 1987): 386-95.

[19]Jean-Luc Martinot et al., "Left Prefrontal Glucose Hypometabolism in the Depressed State: A Confirmation," *American Journal of Psychiatry* 147 (October 1990): 1313-17; Harold A. Sackeim et al., "Regional Cerebral Blood Flow in Mood Disorders," *Archives of General Psychiatry* 47 (January 1990): 60-70.

[20]John M. Booker and Carla J. Hellekson, "Prevalence of Seasonal Affective Disorder in Alaska," *American Journal of Psychiatry* 149 (September 1992): 1176-82.

[21]Susan A. Englund and Daniel N. Klein, "The Genetics of Neurotic-Reactive Depression: A Reanalysis of Shapiro's (1970) Twin Study Using Diagnostic Criteria," *Journal of Affective Disorders* 18 (1990): 247-52; John A. Talbott et al., eds., *Textbook of Psychiatry* (Washington, D.C.: American Psychiatric Press, 1988), p. 49; Svenn Torgersen, "Genetic Factors in Moderately Severe and Mild Affective Disorders," *Archives of General Psychiatry* 43 (March 1986): 222-26.

[22]Nancy C. Andreasen, "Creativity and Mental Illness: Prevalence Rates in Writers

and Their First-Degree Relatives," *American Journal of Psychiatry* 144 (October 1987): 1288-92.

[23] Lester Grinspoon, ed., *Psychiatric Update: The American Psychiatric Association Annual Review* (Washington, D.C.: American Psychiatric Press, 1983), 2:319.

[24] Janice E. Egeland et al., "Special Section: Epidemiologic Study of Affective Disorders Among the Amish," *The American Journal of Psychiatry* 140 (January 1983): 56-71 (some of the data I cite also came from the editorials in this issue, pp. 72-75); John R. Kelsoe et al., "Studies Search for a Gene for Bipolar Affective Disorder in the Old Order Amish," *The Psychiatric Times,* June 1990.

[25] A. Bertelsen et al., "A Danish Twin Study of Manic-Depressive Disorders," *British Journal of Psychiatry* 130 (1977): 330-51; McGuffin et al., "Camberwell Collaborative Depression Study"; Pardes et al., "Genetics and Psychiatry"; Talbott et al., *Textbook of Psychiatry;* Torgersen, "Genetic Factors in Moderately Severe and Mild Affective Disorders," pp. 222-26.

[26] Ernest P. Noble, "Genetic Studies in Alcoholism: CNS Functioning and Molecular Biology," *Psychiatric Annals* 21 (April 1991): 215-29.

[27] Norman S. Miller and John N. Chappel, "History of the Disease Concept," *Psychiatric Annals* 21 (April 1991): 196-205.

[28] Steven M. Mirin and Roger D. Weiss, "Genetic Factors in the Development of Alcoholism," *Psychiatric Annals* 19 (May 1989): 239-42; Marc A. Schuckit, "Two Decades of Alcoholism Genetics Research Reviewed," *The Psychiatric Times: Medicine & Behavior,* February 1990, pp. 39-40; John Wallace, "The New Disease Model of Alcoholism," *The Western Journal of Medicine* 152 (May 1990): 501-5.

[29] E. J. Khantzian, "A Clinical Perspective of the Cause-Consequence Controversy in Alcoholic and Addictive Suffering," *Journal of the American Academy of Psychoanalysis* 15, no. 4 (1987): 521-37.

[30] Roy W. Pickens et al., "Heterogeneity in the Inheritance of Alcoholism," *Archives of General Psychiatry* 48 (January 1991): 19-28.

[31] C. Robert Cloninger, "A Prospective Follow-up and Family Study of Somatization in Men and Women," *American Journal of Psychiatry* 143 (July 1986): 873-78; A. J. Holland et al., "Anorexia Nervosa: A Study of Thirty-four Twin Pairs and One Set of Triplets," *British Journal of Psychiatry* 145 (1984): 414-19; Michael Strober et al., "A Controlled Family Study of Anorexia Nervosa," *Journal of Psychiatric Research* 19, nos. 2/3 (1985): 239-46; Svenn Torgersen, "Genetics of Somatoform Disorders," *Archives of General Psychiatry* 43 (May

1986): 502-5.

Psychosomatic types of illnesses were once called "hysteria" and are now referred to as Briquet's Syndrome or somatization disorder.

[32]Edward R. Ritvo et al., "Concordance for the Syndrome of Autism in Forty Pairs of Afflicted Twins," *American Journal of Psychiatry* 142 (January 1985): 74-77.

[33]Kaplan and Sadock, *Comprehensive Textbook of Psychiatry*, pp. 1774-78, 1830-38; Ronald Pies, "The Biology of Attention-Deficit Disorder," *The Psychiatric Times*, August 1991, pp. 7-11.

[34]"Untangling the Genetic Roots of Mental Disorders," *Clinical Psychiatric News*, April 1990, pp. 2, 20; "Multiple Gene Disorders Are Geneticists' Challenge of the '90s," *The Psychiatric Times*, June 1990 (reprinted from *Science*, March 30, 1990).

Many illnesses are thought to be caused by polygenic factors—that is, the same illness may be caused by several different genetic abnormalities. Atherosclerosis, hypercholesterolemia, Alzheimer's, some cancers, diabetes, mental retardation, manic-depressive illness and schizophrenia all involve a number of genes—just as height and intelligence do.

[35]Joseph Biederman et al., "Evidence of Familial Association Between Attention Deficit Disorder and Major Affective Disorders," *Archives of General Psychiatry* 48 (July 1991): 633-42; Stephen V. Faraone et al., "A Family-Genetic Study of Girls with DSM-III Attention Deficit Disorder," *American Journal of Psychiatry* 148 (January 1991): 112-18.

[36]Elliot S. Gershon et al., "Clinical Findings in Patients with Anorexia Nervosa and Affective Illness in Their Relatives," *American Journal of Psychiatry* 141 (November 1984): 1419-22; Timothy M. Rivinus et al., "Anorexia Nervosa and Affective Disorders: A Controlled Family History Study," *American Journal of Psychiatry* 141 (November 1984): 1414-18.

[37]James I. Hudson et al., "A Controlled Study of Lifetime Prevalence of Affective and Other Psychiatric Disorders in Bulimic Outpatients," *American Journal of Psychiatry* 144 (October 1987); Joy A. Kassett et al., "Psychiatric Disorders in the First-Degree Relatives of Probands with Bulimia Nervosa," *American Journal of Psychiatry* 146 (November 1989): 1468-71; Kenneth S. Kendler et al., "The Genetic Epidemiology of Bulimia Nervosa," *American Journal of Medicine* 148 (December 1991): 1627-37; Camille M. Logue et al., "A Family Study of Anorexia Nervosa and Bulimia," *Comprehensive Psychiatry* 30 (March/April 1989): 179-88.

[38] Svenn Torgersen, "Comorbidity of Major Depression and Anxiety Disorders in Twin Pairs," *American Journal of Psychiatry* 147 (September 1990): 1199-1202; T. W. Uhde et al., "Panic Disorder and Major Depressive Disorder: Biological Relationship," *Biological Psychiatry,* 1985, pp. 88-90.

[39] Kathleen R. Merikangas et al., "Assortative Mating and Affective Disorders: Psychopathology in Offspring," *Psychiatry* 51 (February 1988): 48-56; George Winokur and William Coryell, "Familial Alcoholism in Primary Unipolar Major Depressive Disorder," *American Journal of Psychiatry* 148 (February 1991): 184-88.

[40] Jean Marx, "Dissecting the Complex Diseases," *Science* 247:1540-42.

[41] Myra V. Gormley, "Coming to Grips with Heredity," *Los Angeles Times Magazine,* April 29, 1990.

[42] A. Thomas and S. Chess, *Temperament and Development* (New York: Brunner/Mazel, 1977), quoted in James B. Payton, "Psychic Trauma and Personality Disorders: Nature vs. Nurture," *Highland Highlights* 13, no. 1 (1990): 5-12.

[43] Gavin Andrews et al., "The Genetics of Six Neurotic Disorders: A Twin Study," *Journal of Affective Disorders* 19 (1990): 28.

[44] Thomas J. Bouchard Jr. et al., "Sources of Human Psychological Differences: The Minnesota Study of Twins Reared Apart," *Science* 250 (October 12, 1990): 223-28.

[45] Thomas H. Maugh II, "Study of Twins Emphasizes Importance of Heredity," *Los Angeles Times,* October 12, 1990.

[46] Quote from a participant at the New Orleans meeting of American Association for the Advancement of Science, in Thomas H. Maugh II, "Infant's Ability to Bond with Mother May Be Innate, Psychologist Says," *Los Angeles Times,* February 17, 1990.

[47] J. Wahlstrom, "Inherited Mental Disorders," *Acta Psychiatry Scandinavia* 80 (1989): 111-17.

[48] Howard Fishman, "Illinois Lawsuit Seeks Equal Insurance Coverage for Bipolar Affective Disorder," *The Psychiatric Times* 6 (December 1989): 1.

[49] "California Mandates Parity for Some Mental Disorders," *Psychiatric News,* October 20, 1989, pp. 1, 15.

[50] "New California Law Requires Insurance Coverage for Specific Mental Disorders," *The Psychiatric Times,* January 1990, p. 3.

[51] Samuel B. Guze, "Biological Psychiatry: Is There Any Other Kind?" *Psychological Medicine* 19 (1989): 318.

[52] Quoted in Maugh, "Study of Twins."

Chapter 6: How Childhood Experiences and Stress Cause Emotional Illness

[1]Lenore C. Terr, "Chowchilla Revisited: The Effects of Psychic Trauma Four Years After a School-Bus Kidnapping," *American Journal of Psychiatry* 140 (December 1983): 1543-50; Lenore C. Terr, *Too Scared to Cry* (New York: Harper & Row, 1990).

[2]Shari Roan, "Experts See Adult Effects of Molestation," *Los Angeles Times,* August 7, 1990, pp. E1, E12.

[3]Elaine Hilberman Carmen et al., "Victims of Violence and Psychiatric Illness," *American Journal of Psychiatry* 141 (March 1984): 378-83; Judith L. Herman, "Childhood Trauma in Borderline Personality Disorder," *American Journal of Psychiatry* 146 (April 1989): 490-95; Kaplan and Sadock, *Comprehensive Text-book of Psychiatry,* pp. 1965-68; Thomas H. Maugh II, "Studies Link Childhood Abuse to Adult Social Dysfunction," *Los Angeles Times,* February 17, 1991, p. A5; Susan N. Ogata et al., "Childhood Sexual and Physical Abuse in Adult Patients with Borderline Personality Disorder," *American Journal of Psychiatry* 147 (August 1990): 1008-13; James B. Payton, "Psychic Trauma and Personality Disorders: Nature vs. Nurture," *Highland Highlights* 13, no. 1 (1990): 5-12; Steven L. Shearer et al., "Frequency and Correlates of Childhood Sexual and Physical Abuse Histories in Adult Female Borderline Inpatients," *American Journal of Psychiatry* 147 (February 1990): 214-18; Leonard L. Shengold, "Child Abuse and Deprivation: Soul Murder," *Journal of the American Psychoanalytic Association* 27, no. 3 (1979): 533-59; Lenore C. Terr, "Childhood Traumas: An Outline and Overview," *American Journal of Psychiatry* 148 (January 1991): 10-20.

[4]Judith V. Becker et al., "Sexual Problems of Sexual Assault Survivors," *Women & Health* 9, no. 4 (1984): 5-20; Judith V. Becker et al., "Sequelae of Sexual Assault: The Survivor's Perspective," lecture presented at UCLA conference, August 1990; Ann W. Burgess et al., "Abused to Abuser: Antecedents of Socially Deviant Behaviors," *American Journal of Psychiatry* 144 (November 1987): 1431-36; Jean Goodwin et al., "Borderline and Other Severe Symptoms in Adult Survivors of Incestuous Abuse," *Psychiatric Annals* 20 (January 1990): 21-32; James Morrison, "Childhood Sexual Histories of Women with Somatization Disorder," *American Journal of Psychiatry* 146 (February 1989): 239-41; R. L. Palmer, "Childhood Sexual Experiences with Adults Reported by Women with Eating Disorders: An Extended Series," *British Journal of Psychiatry* 156 (1990): 699-703.

[5]Hagop S. Akiskal, "New Insights into the Nature and Heterogeneity of Mood Disorders," *Journal of Clinical Psychiatry* 50 supp. (May 1989): 6-12; John Bowlby, "Childhood Mourning and Its Implications for Psychiatry," *American Journal of Psychiatry*, December 1961, pp. 481-98; Rene A. Spitz, "Anaclitic Depression: An Inquiry into the Genesis of Psychiatric Conditions in Early Childhood," *Psychoanalytic Study of the Child* (New York: International Universities Press, 1942), 2:313-42.

[6]Alan Breier et al., "Early Parental Loss and Development of Adult Psychopathology," *Archives of General Psychiatry* 45 (November 1988): 987-93.

[7]William R. Beardslee et al., "Children of Parents with Major Affective Disorder: A Review," *American Journal of Psychiatry* 140 (July 1983): 825-32.

[8]Linda Ganzini et al., "Prevalence of Mental Disorders After Catastrophic Financial Loss," *Journal of Nervous and Mental Diseases* 178 (November 1990): 680-85.

[9]Becker et al., "Sequelae of Sexual Assault"; Becker et al., "Sexual Problems of Sexual Assault Survivors"; Jose M. Santiago et al., "Long-Term Psychological Effects of Rape in Thirty-five Rape Victims," *American Journal of Psychiatry* 142 (November 1985): 1338-40; Idee Winfield et al., "Sexual Assault and Psychiatric Disorders Among a Community Sample of Women," *American Journal of Psychiatry* 143 (March 1990): 335-41.

[10]1 Samuel 23; Psalm 22, 31; Job 3, 7, 9—10, 16—17, 19, 30.

[11]Thomas H. Holmes and Richard H. Rahe, "The Social Readjustment Rating Scale," *Journal of Psychosomatic Research* 11 (1967): 213-18.

[12]Paul E. Bebbington and Robin M. Murray, quoted in "Schizophrenia Onset Tied to Life Stresses," *Clinical Psychiatric News,* September 1990, p. 1; Dan Blazer et al., "Stressful Life Events and the Onset of a Generalized Anxiety Syndrome," *American Journal of Psychiatry* 144 (September 1987): 1178-83; C. A. Clifford et al., "Genetic and Environmental Influences on Obsessional Traits and Symptoms," *Psychological Medicine* 14 (1984): 791-800; Deborah S. Cowley and Peter P. Roy-Byrne, "Psychosocial Aspects" [of Panic Disorder], *Psychiatric Annals* 18 (August 1988): 464-67; Aimee Ellicott et al., "Life Events and the Course of Bipolar Disorder," *American Journal of Psychiatry* 147 (September 1990): 1194-98; Carlo Faravelli and Stefano Pallanti, "Recent Life Events and Panic Disorder," *American Journal of Psychiatry* 146 (May 1989): 622-26; Barry Glassner and C. V. Haldipur, "Life Events and Early and Late Onset of Bipolar Disorder," *American Journal of Psychiatry* 140 (February 1983): 215-17; Carlos A. Leon and Agatha Leon, "Panic Disorder and Parental Bonding," *Psychiatric*

Annals 20 (September 1990): 503-8; Jari Miller, "Panic Disorder Is a Combination of Biological and Cognitive Factors," _The Psychiatric Times_ 7 (April 1990): 1.

[13]"Groups Revise Definition of Alcoholism to Reflect Recent Research Advances," _Psychiatric News,_ June 1, 1990 (presentation from a joint committee of the American Society of Addiction Medicine and the National Council on Alcoholism and Drug Dependence).

[14]MacArthur, _Our Sufficiency in Christ,_ p. 77.

[15]Hunt, _Beyond Seduction,_ p. 127.

[16]Ibid, p. 206.

Chapter 7: What About Personal Choice?

[1]"Precursors of Affective Illness May Be Detectable in Infants 12-15 Months," _Clinical Psychiatry News,_ February 1987.

[2]Glasser, _Reality Therapy._

[3]Bainton, _Here I Stand,_ pp. 362-63.

Chapter 8: Putting It All Together

[1]_The Psychiatric Times: Medicine & Behavior,_ September 1990, p. 80.

[2]David Rowe, quoted in Maugh, "Study of Twins," p. A40.

[3]William Glasser, _Take Effective Control of Your Life_ (New York: Harper & Row, 1984).

[4]Khantzian, "A Clinical Perspective of the Cause-Consequence Controversy," pp. 522-25.

[5]Deborah S. Pinkney, "Specialists Give New Definition of Alcoholism," _American Medical News,_ May 11, 1990.

[6]Maristela G. Monteiro and Marc A. Schuckit, "Populations at High Alcoholism Risk: Recent Findings," _Journal of Clinical Psychiatry_ 49 supp. (September 1988): 5.

[7]"Evidence Seen for Genetic Link in Schizophrenia," _Psychiatric News,_ December 1988, p. 14.

[8]Humble, "Aetiology and Mechanisms of Anxiety Disorders."

[9]Kenneth S. Kendler, "Overview: A Current Perspective on Twin Studies of Schizophrenia," _American Journal of Psychiatry_ 140 (November 1983): 1413-25. This article shows evidence that, on the average, 68 percent of the cause of schizophrenia is genetic factors. That is compared to a 75 percent genetic cause for diabetes mellitus and 57 percent for hypertension.

Chapter 9: The Church: Business, School or Hospital?

[1]Henry Cloud, *When Your World Makes No Sense* (Nashville: Thomas Nelson, 1990), p. 38.

[2]Dietrich Bonhoeffer, *Life Together* (London: SCM Press, 1954), pp. 100-101.

[3]Ibid.

[4]Hunt, *Beyond Seduction*, pp. 117, 144-45.

[5]MacArthur, *Our Sufficiency in Christ*, pp. 75-76.

[6]Alan Breier and John S. Strauss, "The Role of Social Relationships in the Recovery from Psychotic Disorders," *American Journal of Psychiatry* 141 (August 1984): 949-55.

[7]These seven points come from Richard L. Leavy, "Social Support and Psychological Disorder: A Review," *Journal of Community Psychology* 11 (January 1983): 3-21.

[8]Joseph M. Stowell, "Front Lines," *Moody Monthly*, May 1991, p. 4.

Chapter 10: How the Strong Can Help—Not Shoot—the Wounded

[1]Paul Tournier, *The Strong and the Weak* (Philadelphia: Westminster Press, 1963), pp. 20-21.

[2]Wanamaker, *The Epistles to the Thessalonians*.

[3]Best, *A Commentary on the First and Second Epistles to the Thessalonians*, p. 232.

Chapter 11: What the Wounded Can Do While the Bullets Are Flying

[1]J. Gartner et al., "Religious Commitment and Mental Health: A Review of the Empirical Literature," *Journal of Psychology and Theology* 19 (1991): 6-25; H. G. Koenig et al., "Religious Coping and Depression Among Elderly, Hospitalized Medically Men," *American Journal of Psychiatry* 149 (December 1992): 1693-1700; David B. Larson et al., "Associations Between Dimensions of Religious Commitment and Mental Health Reported in the *American Journal of Psychiatry* and *Archives of General Psychiatry:* 1978-1989," *American Journal of Psychiatry* 149 (April 1992): 557-59; L. R. Peterson and A. Roy, "Religiosity, Anxiety, and Meaning and Purpose: Religion's Consequences for Psychological Well-Being," *Review of Religious Research* 27 (September 1985): 49-62; Peter Pressman et al., "Religious Belief, Depression and Ambulation Status in Elderly Women with Broken Hips," *American Journal of Psychiatry* 147 (June 1990): 758-60; K. A. Sherril and D. B. Larson, "Adult Burn Patients: The Role of Religion in Recovery," *South Medical Journal* 81 (1988): 821-29;

F. D. Willits and D. M. Crider, "Religion and Well-Being: Men and Women in the Middle Years," *Review of Religious Research* 29 (1988): 281-92.

[2]Paul Brand and Philip Yancey, *Fearfully and Wonderfully Made* (Grand Rapids, Mich.: Zondervan, 1980), p. 105.

[3]C. A. H. Watts, "A Long-Term Follow-up of Schizophrenic Patients: 1946-1983," *Journal of Clinical Psychiatry* 46 (June 1985): 210-16.

[4]Courtenay M. Harding et al., "The Vermont Longitudinal Study of Persons with Severe Mental Illness: Part 1, Methodology, Study Sample and Overall Status Thirty-two Years Later," *American Journal of Psychiatry* 144 (June 1987): 718-26.

[5]"Treatment Will Lessen Suffering, Yield Significant Cost Savings," *Psychiatric News,* April 16, 1993, p. 4. Data was extracted by the National Institutes of Mental Health from a report prepared by the NIMH's advisory council on the cost and treatment of severe mental illness.

[6]Anne Huffman, "God Has a Market for Cracked Pots," talk recorded at the Rolling Hills Women's Retreat, Alpine Covenant Conference Center, Blue Jay, California, April 1991.

Appendix

[1]Sid Macaulay, "No Ax to Grind," *Psychiatry Section Newsletter* (Christian Medical & Dental Society), December 1989, pp. 3-4.

[2]In extremely rare situations, when a person threatens society, he may be forced to take medication against his wishes. However, this can occur only under the jurisdiction of the courts and probably accounts for less than one in five million doses of psychotropic medications prescribed.

[3]Sorosky, *Handbook of Modern Psychopharmacology,* pp. 143-47, 177.

[4]Eric D. Peselow et al., "Dysfunctional Attitudes in Depressed Patients Before and After Clinical Treatment and in Normal Control Subjects," *American Journal of Psychiatry* 147 (April 1990): 439-44.

[5]Jonathan R. T. Davidson, "Continuation Treatment of Panic Disorder with High-Potency Benzodiazepines," *Journal of Clinical Psychiatry* 51, supp. A (December 1990): 31-37.

[6]Steven L. Dubovsky, "Generalized Anxiety Disorders: New Concepts and Psychopharmacologic Therapies," *Journal of Clinical Psychiatry* 51 supp. (January 1990): 3-10.

[7]"Experts Issue Guidelines on Benzodiazepines," Report of the APA Task Force APA-90, *Clinical Perspectives* 3, no. 5 (1990): 1-4.